Missing Organizational Linkages

FOUNDATIONS FOR ORGANIZATIONAL SCIENCE
A Sage Publications Series

Series Editor

David Whetten, *Brigham Young University*

Editors

Peter J. Frost, *University of British Columbia*
Anne S. Huff, *University of Colorado* and *Cranfield University* (UK)
Benjamin Schneider, *University of Maryland*
M. Susan Taylor, *University of Maryland*
Andrew Van de Ven, *University of Minnesota*

The FOUNDATIONS FOR ORGANIZATIONAL SCIENCE series supports the development of students, faculty, and prospective organizational science professionals through the publication of texts authored by leading organizational scientists. Each volume provides a highly personal, hands-on introduction to a core topic or theory and challenges the reader to explore promising avenues for future theory development and empirical application.

Books in This Series

Paul S. Goodman

Missing Organizational Linkages

Tools for Cross-Level Research

Foundations for
Organizational
Science
A Sage Publications Series

Sage Publications, Inc.
International Educational and Professional Publisher
Thousand Oaks ▪ London ▪ New Delhi

For information:

Sage Publications, Inc.
2455 Teller Road
Thousand Oaks, California 91320
E-mail: order@sagepub.com

Sage Publications Ltd.
6 Bonhill Street
London EC2A 4PU
United Kingdom

Sage Publications India Pvt. Ltd.
M-32 Market
Greater Kailash I
New Delhi 110 048 India

Printed in the United States of America

Library of Congress Cataloging-in-Publication Data

Goodman, Paul S.
  Missing organizational linkages: Tools for cross-level research / by
Paul S. Goodman.
      p. cm. — (Foundations for organizational science)
  Includes bibliographical references and index.
  ISBN 0-7619-1617-2 (acid-free paper) — ISBN 0-7619-1618-0 (pbk. :
acid-free paper)
  1. Industrial productivity. 2. Organizational effectiveness. I. Title. II. Series.
  HD56 .G664 2000
  658.4'02—dc21   00-008798

This book is printed on acid-free paper.

00 01 02 03 04 05 06 7 6 5 4 3 2 1

Acquisition Editor:	Marquita Flemming
Editorial Assistant:	Mary Ann Vail
Production Editor:	Astrid Virding
Editorial Assistant:	Candice Crosetti
Typesetter:	Danielle Dillahunt

Contents

Introduction to the Series

The title of this series, **Foundations for Organizational Science** (FOS), denotes a distinctive focus. FOS books are educational aids for mastering the core theories, essential tools, and emerging perspectives that constitute the field of organizational science (broadly conceived to include organizational behavior, organizational theory, human resource management, and business strategy). Our ambitious goal is to assemble the "essential library" for members of our professional community.

The vision for the series emerged from conversations with several colleagues, including Peter Frost, Anne Huff, Rick Mowday, Ben Schneider, Susan Taylor, and Andy Van de Ven. A number of common interests emerged from these sympathetic encounters, including: enhancing the quality of doctoral education by providing broader access to the master teachers in our field, "bottling" the experience and insights of some of the founding scholars in our field before they retire, and providing professional development opportunities for colleagues seeking to broaden their u nderstanding of the rapidly expanding subfields within organizational science.

Our unique learning objectives are reflected in an unusual set of instructions to FOS authors. They are encouraged to: (1) "write the way they teach"—framing their book as an extension of their teaching notes, rather than as the expansion of a handbook chapter; (2) pass on their "craft knowledge" to the next generation of scholars—making them wiser, not just smarter; (3) share with their "virtual students and colleagues" the insider tips and best-bets for research that are normally reserved for one-on-one mentoring sessions; and (4) make the complexity of their subject matter comprehensible to non-experts so that readers can share their puzzlement, fascination, and intrigue.

We are proud of the group of highly qualified authors who have embraced the unique educational perspective of our "Foundations" series. We encourage your suggestions for how these books can better satisfy your learning needs—as a newcomer to the field preparing for prelims or developing a dissertation proposal, or as an established scholar seeking to broaden your knowledge and proficiency.

—DAVID A. WHETTEN
SERIES EDITOR

Preface

I had the privilege of working with the Human Factors Committee of the National Research Council for more than 7 years. Composed of a group of experts from many fields and with diverse interests, the committee organizes its work around projects that, in most cases, become books or reports.

My first encounter with the committee was on a project on the productivity paradox headed by Doug Harris. The paradox basically asserts that investments in information technology designed to enhance productivity have not increased productivity. This is a nice problem because although information technology pervades our lives and appears to make things better, a variety of empirical evidence suggests the investments have had little effect. A group of us—Bob Pritchard, Dave Whetten, Ben Schneider, and John Campbell, to name a few—got together periodically to think about this paradox.

Now, at one level, for organizational scholars interested in technology, the explanation for "no effects" can be tied to "poor implementations." There is a very large literature on implementations of change that indicates that many are failures. The poor implementation argument is one way to account for the productivity paradox, but that is too easy. The other explanation is much more challenging. The technology was successfully implemented, and it produced productivity enhancements at the individual or group levels, but not at the organizational level. That is a more interesting and harder question. We all played with approaches to understanding the paradox, and the results appeared in a 1994 publication by the NRC titled "Organizational Linkages."

Although over my career I have written about different aspects of organizational effectiveness, this was my first time exploring the linkage question. All the contributors to the book, including myself, had discovered some conceptual tools, but there were many unanswered questions. So, when the opportunity to write a book in this series presented itself, building a better understanding about organizational linkages seemed a natural next step. In most of the books I have written, the topic was on something I had been working on for some time. It was about something well rehearsed. For this book, the challenge was different. Organizational linkages is a relatively new research area. Although I legitimate this point in the body of the book, there is not very much theoretical or empirical work on this topic. Thus, the intellectual task is to define a new area conceptually rather than to synthesize and advance a well-established area. That has been an exciting challenge.

Given that the book explores a new area, I have written in more of an informal and conversational mode. I really want to engage you in a conversation. Indeed, all the chapters but the final one conclude with a conversation. Also, after you have read the book, I provide a Web site for further conversations.

We all believe that context makes a difference in studying work organizations. The same is true for this book. I wrote the book in a beautiful home located in Harpswell, Maine. The house sits directly over the water. The multiple windows provide a very broad, panoramic view of the Casco Bay—the rocks, the islands, the fog, and so forth. My wife, Denise Rousseau, and I rent this setting for book writing. We only go off-season when the only inhabitants are the lobsters and a few lobstermen. It is quite a beautiful surrounding where one can think, write, revise, and rethink.

Another part of context is people. Denise was a great supporter throughout the writing. She possesses a great set of skills, which ranges from helping me to spell correctly (she went to Catholic grammar school and I didn't) to navigating and creating the conceptual ideas tied around linkages. She also has been a greater supporter of the idea for the book.

In addition to the conversations in Harpswell, many other people contributed to this undertaking. Ben Schneider was a strong supporter of the book and read and commented on drafts. I corralled other people, such as Jim Dean and Jeanne Wilson, to read other sections. I tried to read and gather information broadly. Jacobo Bielak from Carnegie

Mellon's engineering school gave me a primer on earthquakes, particularly the timing of these phenomena. Bill Brown, the head of our biology department, also provided some instruction on levels of analysis in his discipline. I have worked a great deal with Ranga Ramanujam on organizational errors. Lots of our joint collaboration appears in Chapter 5.

The production, which means typing, footnotes, and all those other details, was done spectacularly by Bernie Leppold. Bernie is a jewel. Judy Leppold did a great job as my editor of the manuscript.

The book is dedicated to my brother, Richard, who was very smart, quite funny, and a pretty good pool player.

1 Beginning the Conversation

This book is the beginning of a conversation about organizational linkages. *Organizational linkages* is not a well-delineated concept in organizational science. In contrast to concepts such as organizational culture, groups, or institutional theory, organizational linkage does not yet have a developed literature, with controversies that have ebbed and flowed. Organizational linkages is more at its beginning. Thus, this is not a retrospective about what we have learned. Rather, this book is a prospective piece. I discuss, explore, ask questions, identify, and recognize some common organizational mysteries and engage you in a conversation as you have touched a part or whole of this book.

You will see right away that this book has an informal tone. It is written differently from other books I have written or from other books in our field. It is not structured with a formal problem statement, literature review, model, and applications. Rather, there is a strong focus on building stories that the reader and I can use for points of discussion. Some concepts are presented earlier, but others are introduced throughout the book. The idea of a conversation is taken literally, in that each chapter ends with a conversation between me and an imaginary you. Also, there is a Web site for the book to continue the conversation.

The following four stories create pictures of activities and outcomes occurring at one level that have consequences for another level or unit. In one sense, that is the essence of organizational linkages. Consider the following case.

Case 1A: Barings

The chairman of Barings, a 233-year-old British investment bank, announced in February 1995 that his organization was filing for bankruptcy. A trader in the bank's Singapore office had accumulated $1.3 billion in unrecoverable losses. An investigation by the government of Singapore indicated that the bank's collapse could have been avoided, and suggested that the collapse was caused by "institutional incompetence or lack of understanding of business among senior executives and a total failure of internal controls" (Ministry of Finance Report, 1995, p. 1) There also happened to be an earthquake in Kobe, Japan, that affected (lowered) stock prices and exposed the bank to huge losses because of the trader's position.

An organizational linkage perspective focuses on how and why these activities and consequences occurred. How are activities and outcomes at one level connected to activities and outcomes at another level? Why was the trader permitted to both trade and settle accounts after an internal audit report recommended that this practice be discontinued? There were clear rules concerning what were authorized and unauthorized trades. Also, there were measurement systems to monitor trades. Why did he continue unauthorized trades? How did these events and outcomes at one level bring down a bank that had been in existence for more than 200 years?

Case 1B: Allied Manufacturing—Teams

The president at Allied Manufacturing was a strong supporter of the use of self-designing teams in production settings. A major system-wide change program was introduced in Allied's Ohio plant. The plant was organized around teams that were responsible for scheduling work, assigning personnel, conducting inspections, and performing other related activities. Extensive training, overtime, reconfiguration of the technical system, and pay-for-knowledge systems were introduced to support the team-based initiative. A year after the introduction of this system-wide change, measures of group-level quality and productivity were up significantly. However, there were no comparable changes in quality, productivity, and other performance indicators at the organizational level at Allied Manufacturing.

This is a nice example of an organizational linkage problem, a case in which there are demonstrable changes in outcomes at one level but not at another level. The motivation for this organizational change was not just to benefit the employees or work groups. The underlying assumption was that positive benefits to groups would lead to positive benefits or outcomes for the organization. An organizational linkage perspective "traces out" how and why observable changes at the group level did or did not appear at the organizational level.

Case 1C: Retailer—Downsizing

The top management of a major retailer decides that to remain competitive, it must reduce the number of employees. A 15% reduction is planned, with the expectation of lowering costs and increasing productivity. The reduction is implemented across the board for exempt and nonexempt personnel at their 50 stores and central office. A year after the change, labor costs at the organizational level have declined, but much less than expected. Also, in marked contrast to expectations, individual productivity, which is well measured in this environment, had substantially declined.

An organizational linkage approach focuses on how changes in one level have an impact on other levels. In this example, organizational-level changes were associated with declines in individual-level productivity. What are the conditions when downsizing will decrease or increase individual-level productivity?

Case 1D: Product Design and Manufacturing

A product design group in a manufacturing organization recently purchased and effectively implemented a new computer-aided design (CAD) software system, which has increased substantially the group's capability to create new product designs for the downstream manufacturing organization. A year after the acquisition of the CAD technology, the manufacturing group still produced the same products that it had in the past.

An organizational linkage approach can focus on horizontal as well as vertical changes. In this example, increases in the outcomes of the design group (i.e., number of new products designed) did not lead to the production of new products by the manufacturing group. The previous examples portrayed how changes at one level (e.g., the group) did or did not affect outcomes at another level (e.g., the organization). Tracing out changes in activities and outcomes of one unit on another is a basic task of organizational linkage analysis. The units may be arranged vertically, horizontally, or in some other organizational space.

These four examples are a brief introduction to linkages and possess some common features. First, there is a focus on the interrelations among organizational levels or units. The examples included individual, group, and organizational hierarchical levels, as well as interrelations between organizational units (e.g., design and manufacturing). Second, they focus on how activities and outcomes at one level are connected to activities and outcomes at a different level. The key element in organizational linkage analysis is to explain how changes in activities and outcomes at one level (e.g., the self-designing team example) or unit are linked to changes (or no changes) at another level or unit in a specified time period or over multiple time periods. Third, although not explicit in the examples, the goal of organizational linkage analysis is to specify the conditions and mechanisms when activities and outcomes at one level (e.g., the trader in the Barings example) will or will not change the activities and outcomes at another level or unit.

These examples also suggest what organizational linkage is not about. We are not interested in why a trader exceeded the trading limits. Rather, we are interested in the conditions and mechanisms that permitted this trading behavior to lead to bankruptcy. Similarly, we are not interested in how and why self-designing teams may lead to increases in group productivity or quality. Rather, we take the changes in group outcomes as a given and ask whether these group-level changes will benefit the organization. This, of course, was the assumption in introducing self-designing teams, but the assumption is rarely tested theoretically or empirically.

In the case of the new CAD, the typical research focus is how to implement that technology successfully and how to assess its impact on the productivity of the design group. We start with the assumption that the technology is successfully implemented and it has demonstrated positive effects on the design process, that is, our strategy is asking whether increased productivity of the design group affects the work of manufacturing. By focusing on the relations between outcomes across units or levels, we are not suggesting that prior questions are trivial. Understanding and improving team productivity is a hard problem.

Successfully implementing new technology and assessing its impact is also a hard problem. There are many unanswered theoretical and methodological questions. But our attention is on exploring a critical assumption that has not received much attention. If we can demonstrate positive effects of work group design or the introduction of new technology, will they have effects on outcomes at other levels or units? We tend to assume it will but rarely develop the tools to test this assumption theoretically or empirically.

The goals of this book, then, are the following. I want to delineate the concept of organizational linkages, draw some preliminary boundaries around the topic, describe its distinctive features, and explain how they differ from other concepts in the literature. The second goal is to present some tools for you. The tools could be used to make sense of these and other organizational stories in this book. Or you might be structuring some organizational work, and the tools might provide a new way to frame the problem, see activities and outcomes in different ways, and reorganize your thinking in certain established areas in the literature.

To explore organizational linkages, it is necessary to ground the concept in real organizational phenomena. Sailing only in very abstract waters would be a disservice to the reader and myself. I have selected three areas—organizational change, organizational errors, and organizational learning. Why these three? Primarily because they are areas in which I have worked and because I have lots of very concrete organizational images. Second, these are important organizational areas of current interest in the field, and they are inherently multilevel in nature. The literature on organizational change (Argyris, 1985, 1990; Lawler, 1986, 1996; Lawler, Mohrman, & Ledford, 1998; Nadler, Gerstein, & Shaw, 1992; Nadler, Shaw, & Walton, 1995) has been a dominant area in organizational research for some time. The work on organization errors (Perrow, 1984; Roberts, 1990), sometimes framed in terms of "high reliability organizations," and organizational learning (Argote, 1999; Huber, 1991; March, 1991; Miner & Mezias, 1996) are emerging and significant areas in our field. These are areas that have been and will continue to be important in organizational science. They also represent areas in which I have worked conceptually and in field settings.

My strategy, then, is to explore the concept of organizational linkages and then apply it to the three cited areas. This application will sharpen the concept and illustrate common elements of organizational linkages across all three areas as well as highlight their differences. Thinking about the linkage concept across change, errors, and learning also presents gaps in our understanding. The gaps may be mysteries, or they may be solvable by you or others. At the conclusion of this book, I hope you will be excited to extend linkage analysis beyond these three intellectual areas.

Rationale

I intend to provide some fairly simple rationales for paying attention to organizational linkages. As this analysis unfolds, I hope other compelling arguments will come to the surface.

The first rationale is that the organizational linkage perspective provides a new way to think about multilevel organizational phenomena. Our field traditionally has specialized by levels of analysis. For example, one can be a groups person or an organizational ecologist. Our research, how we train each new generation of researchers, and our professional associations display a clear level bias, that is, we tend to focus on one level of analysis and implicitly make assumptions about the relation between the focal unit and other units of analysis. In contrast to prevailing practices in organizational research, this book makes explicit these assumptions about interrelations between organizational levels and units.

Let me give you a personal example. A long time ago, I wrote a book titled *Assessing Organizational Change: The Rushton Quality of Work Experiment* (Goodman, 1979). It was a large interdisciplinary effort, assessing the effects of an organizational change project built around self-designing teams. We used tools from econometrics and cost-benefit analysis to more traditional survey methods to trace out the effects of the change. And we did show that this major innovation created positive consequences for productivity, costs, and safety at the group level. During that 3-year adventure, I remember one member of our team asking me if this change benefited the organization. I heard the question but was so locked into the group as a unit of analysis that I just finessed it. Yet, it was the right question. My assumption at the time, and the assumption of many others then and now, was that increasing the effectiveness of teams would improve the effectiveness of the organization. But I never directly tested that assumption. Still, today, many who think about changes in selection, training, reward systems, and many other components of organizations continue to assume that there is a linkage between their interventions at some organizational level and the consequences for the organization. However, this assumption about linkages has not been examined or understood. My goal is to enhance our understanding of linkages for theoretical and practical purposes.

The second rationale for this book is that it extends existing research and provides some new points of convergence between different literature streams. The linkage perspective is a natural outgrowth of the literature on multiple levels that began more than 20 years ago in books such as the one by Roberts, Hulin, and Rousseau (1978). It complements and extends more contemporary advocacy for meso perspectives in organizational research (Rousseau & House, 1994). There are recent multilevel perspectives on group (cf. Hollenbeck, Ilgen, LePine, Colquitt, & Hedlund, 1998) and organizational research (Boning, Ichniowski, & Shaw, 1998; Ichniowski & Shaw, 1999; Lawler et al., 1998), which have ties to organizational linkages. The areas of organizational errors and organizational change are application areas for this book, that is, I use linkage analysis to indicate new perspectives and new research problems with these domain areas. The next section in this chapter sharpens the organizational linkage concept by showing it is complementary to and distinctive from these literatures.

A third rationale for the organizational linkage perspective is relevancy for issues of policy and practice. Consider the concept of the "productivity paradox." Basically, this paradox asserts that countries such as the United States have made huge investments in advanced technologies to improve productivity, but the returns are not commensurate with the investments (Attewell, 1994; Harris, 1994). An important question is why has this paradox occurred? It has far-reaching implications for long-term economic development and the quality of life. At an organizational level, it means that a company invests in information technology, for example, designed to improve productivity and quality, but there are no increases in productivity or quality. One quick resolution to this paradox is simply that the technology is defective, or it was poorly implemented. We all know instances of these two expla-

nations. But think of the scenario in which the technology should increase productivity and quality, and the implementation is actually effective. Why, in such a case, is there no relation between the investment,
organizational changes, and the desired outcomes? This is what the
productivity paradox is really about. The organizational linkage concept is one way to unravel this paradox. The linkage concept can provide some insight on why successful implementation of new information technologies can benefit certain organizational units but not the
organization as a whole.

In addition to broad national concerns, the linkage concept may provide some new ways to frame some existing problems of organizational practice. This chapter opened with cases on four critical topics—
organizational errors, organizational change, downsizing, and the
design-manufacturing interface problem. These are relevant issues in
organizational life. There has been good work done in understanding
these phenomena. The organizational linkage concept can provide new
lenses to deal more effectively with these four areas and, more generally, to identify ways to improve organizational practice.

The final rationale is that forms of organizing are changing. There
are clear movements from working in the same place and time in a formal organization with hierarchical structure to working in environments distributed in space and time with employees from different organizations and with mixes of permanent and contingent workers.

In the next chapter, we explore productivity changes across levels in a
relatively simple, traditional organization. However, the reader should
immediately sense the complexity of tracing outcome changes in this
environment. We also explore the linkage concept in newer ways of organizing. For example, in the next chapter, we consider the crash of
ValuJet Flight 592. The practice of outsourcing many traditional in-
house activities captures one element of new forms of organizing. In
the ValuJet case, the organizational context is formed by the airline and
SabreTech, the company performing maintenance work. There are
clearly other emerging organizational forms such as the networked and
virtual organizations.

The basic argument is that we need to understand the linkage concept in traditional and new forms of organizing. In the context of traditional organizations, we are just beginning to think in linkage terms
(Harris, 1994).

Points of Convergence and Divergence— Existing Literatures

I opened this conversation with an assertion that organizational linkages is not a well-developed concept in organizational science. To develop this argument, I want to begin by briefly pointing to areas of convergence and divergence with existing literatures. One basic task of this book is to sharpen the concept of organizational linkages and demonstrate its conceptual value.

Levels Research

The book by Roberts et al. (1978) marked the beginning of an important discussion on organizational research. Subsequent versions of this line of reasoning have focused our attention on the various meanings of levels and the implications for moving across them. Topics such as aggregation bias and cross-level fallacies mark this literature and provide useful guidelines for researchers working in multilevel systems. For example, work by Klein, Dansereau, and Hall (1994) examined the process of specifying levels of theory, measurement, and analysis in terms of homogeneity, independence, and heterogeneity. Chan's (1998) work provided new insights into conceptual and methodological issues. All these efforts are designed to sharpen our theoretical and methodological approaches to multilevel phenomena.

Our work builds on this literature in the following ways: We want to begin with a clear specification of what we mean theoretically by being at the group level or the organizational level. We want to be careful that using concepts at one level, such as learning, has similar meanings at other levels. Given this intellectual beginning, we move to our principal focus, which is whether changes in group learning and group outcomes, for example, affect or change individual or organizational activities and outcomes.

Meso Research

A related literature advocates a "meso" perspective to organizations (Rousseau & House, 1994). The basic argument in this literature is to pay attention to context, particularly among different levels of analysis. If you are interested in individual behavior and that behavior is displayed in a group context, the nature of the structure within the group will shape individual behavior. In a loosely structured group context, we would expect to see strong variation in individual behavior. Or students of group behavior may want to explore the degree to which the group is embedded in the larger organization. If groups operate in an organizational environment with highly structured performance programs and clearly defined culture and norms, we would expect little variation in group activities. Examining these cross-level effects in different directions (e.g., lower to higher level and with main and interactive effects) is one of the distinguishing features of the meso approach.

This book builds off the meso approach in a number of ways. We are clearly interested in multilevel phenomena and the role of context. Our emphasis diverges in its focus primarily on outcomes. We want to trace changes of outcomes at one level or unit on another. If system-wide changes lead to outcome changes at the group level, we want to understand the mechanisms that explain why group-level outcomes will or will not change organizational outcomes. If learning occurs at a unit level (e.g., a plant) and there are subsequent productivity improvements, we want a methodology to trace out these unit changes on individual-, group-, or corporate-level productivity. Our interest is not on whether learning has the same meaning across levels or whether context makes a difference. (Context does.) Rather, the focus is on the impact of learning on changes in outcome across levels or units.

Multiple Level Perspectives

There is a recent body of research (Hollenbeck et al., 1998) using a multilevel perspective to understand group effectiveness. For example, Hollenbeck et al. (1998) developed a theory that focuses on individual, dyadic, and group decision accuracy. Experience of the group as well as feedback systems also are hypothesized to affect group effectiveness. In a series of laboratory studies, Hollenbeck and his colleagues were able to estimate multilevel predictors of group performance.

I acknowledge the importance of multilevel predictors in understanding groups. However, we take group effectiveness or changes in group effectiveness as our starting point. If feedback systems improve group accuracy, our interest is on the effects of improved accuracy on activities and outcomes of the unit or system in which the group is embedded. If we translate Hollenbeck et al.'s (1998) study into an organizational setting, the question is how improvements in assessing environment or market changes lead to changes in new product development, revenue, or profitability at the organizational level.

In other multilevel research, there are investigations (Ichniowski & Shaw, 1999; Lawler et al., 1998) into how human resources (HR) systems affect firm performance. Practices such as problem-solving teams, extensive orientation, information sharing, and employment security are related to firm performance. Other research (Cascio, Young, & Morris, 1997; Freeman & Cameron, 1993) focuses on how other HR practices such as downsizing affect firm performance. In all these studies, there are implicit assumptions on how HR practices affect individual, group, and organizational practices.

The linkage approach begins with the proposition that multilevel practices can improve firm performance. This approach differs in its focus. If employee orientation, job rotation, or providing extensive market information lead to improvements in individual-level performance, linkage analysis seeks to understand the conditions in which individual performance will or will not contribute to organizational performance. As linkage analysis makes clear, the conditions in which changes in individual performance will lead to changes in organizational-level performance are not obvious.

Errors, Change, and Learning

Previously, I mentioned that the linkage approach would be applied to three current organizational literatures—organizational errors, change, and learning. My strategy is to acknowledge the current work in that area. For example, in the organizational error literature, the contributions of scholars such as Perrow (1984) and Roberts (1990) have provided very different theoretical perspectives in understanding errors. In this book, I analyze two cases—the Barings Bank failure and the ValuJet tragedy. The goal is to show how the linkage approach complements and extends current thinking on organizational errors. The same strategy is used in this book with the literature on organizational change and organizational learning. Using conceptual tools for linkage analysis on real organizational cases, I point to how we complement and extend other literatures.

Systems Dynamics

Other literature streams are introduced in this book. Some, such as the "systems dynamics" perspective, will be less familiar to some organizational researchers. This particular literature (Sterman, 1994; Sterman, Repenning, & Kofman, 1997) is particularly important because of its focus on dynamic mechanisms for understanding changes in organizations. Concepts such as positive and negative feedback cycles, nonlinear changes, and lag structures are all important in understanding how activities and outcomes at one level or unit affect activities and outcomes at different levels or units. One underlying goal for this book is to extend existing literatures and provide new points of convergence between different literatures.

The Road Map

The next two chapters set the stage for analyzing the three content areas. Chapter 2 attempts to ground the reader in the organizational linkage concept by presenting some new stories critical for understanding this concept. The next chapter builds the initial conceptual toolbox. The concepts of outcome coupling and positive and negative feedback systems are introduced. These conceptual tools, then, are applied in Chapter 4—Organizational Errors—to explore why a 200-year-old prestigious bank went bankrupt and why a flight crashed in the Florida Everglades, with all the passengers and crew losing their lives.

The next three chapters deal with linkages and organizational change. That does not mean I think this is a more important area. Rather, it was one logical way to organize the analysis. Chapter 5 explores why successful changes at one level or unit do not affect other levels or units. The concept of "limiting conditions" is introduced to explain this phenomenon. Chapter 6 explores the impact of organizational level (e.g., plant) changes, both on groups and individuals, as well as plant-level changes on corporate-level changes. One question addressed is, how do changes in plant level activities and outcomes affect corporate activities and outcomes?

The last chapter on change focuses on the interrelation among changes in outcomes over time. We explore the organizational improvement paradox, which addresses how positive outcomes lead to negative unanticipated outcomes over the life of a change process.

In Chapter 8, we apply the conceptual tools to learning in organizations. Given a setting in which learning enhances outcomes in a particular unit or level, we trace whether these changes in activities and outcomes will change activities and outcomes in other units or levels. The final chapter captures some of the things we have learned, unresolved issues, and future research challenges.

Concluding Thoughts

- Our basic question is: How are changes in activities and outcomes at one unit or level of analysis related to changes in activities, events, and outcomes at other units or levels of analysis?
- This is a prospective adventure. There are not 10, 20, or 30 years of a cumulative literature on organizational linkages. Our focus is to explore, to look ahead, and to indicate future opportunities.
- At the same time, there are ties to many literatures that are developed throughout the book. The levels literature, work on system dynamics, and Thompson's (1967) concept of interdependence all contribute to our understanding of linkages. As this conversation develops, both the ties to and the differences between the linkage concept and other literatures will be explicit.
- The boundaries of our exploration, to some extent, are defined by the three areas—organizational change, organizational errors, and organizational learning. These areas represent the data or concrete representations for thinking about linkages. Also, my personal focus in these areas has been at or within the organization. It is clear that understanding linkages across other levels also is important.

Conversation One

We said this is a conversation, and conversation means there is at least a two-way exchange. I address this in two ways. First,

You: I still do not understand what you mean by organizational linkages.

PSG: Think about the four examples. That should give you a first approximation. In the Barings case, errors were occurring at the trader level. One interesting question is: How did these individual-level activities and outcomes bring down a 200-year-old institution? What were the mechanisms that permitted this to happen? That is the focus of organizational linkage analysis.

You: But the Barings example is very different from the other examples.

PSG: That is true. Barings and the Allied Manufacturing case are very different. One is about errors and the other is about creating self-designing teams. But there is a common question. How do activities and outcomes at one level affect activities and outcomes at other levels? And that is the basic question of the book.

You: You seem to be claiming too much. Is the linkage concept really new?

PSG: I strongly believe it is a new perspective. Clearly, it is tied to other literatures. I have said that and will make the ties to other literatures as we move through the book. But I am trying to make explicit what we tend to treat implicitly. If we introduce new information technology to improve a unit's effectiveness, we assume that it will benefit individuals, the unit, and the organization. We start our analysis when unit effectiveness is observed, and then try to understand and to trace these outcomes on other units or levels of analysis. I think the difference between linkage and other analyses will be sharper, particularly when we examine Chapters 4 through 8.

Second, there is a Web site set up for this book. The address is http://www.gsia.cmu.edu/afs/andrew/gsia/www/mol/index.html The site includes actual conversations that occurred in the making of the book, some references, and other relevant issues I could not fit in this book. The Web site is also dynamic in that it invites you to respond, and I will try to answer.

2 Framing the Organizational Linkage Problem

This chapter is organized around two organizational stories—one dealing with change and the other with organizational errors. My strategy is clearly to start this book in a more inductive way. I want to immerse the reader in some details of organizational life, and then begin to abstract some elements for our organizational linkage tool kit. The stories, which are much more detailed than the snapshots in Chapter 1, are the data for building the conceptual tools. The idea of storytelling as a fundamental mechanism for learning has been acknowledged by researchers such as Brown and Duguid (1991). I am trying to embed this mechanism early in this book because the linkage concept is relatively new and not well developed in our literature.

At the end of this chapter, the reader should (a) be familiar with two stories that we reference throughout the book, (b) identify some of the basic concepts in linkage analysis, and (c) recognize ties to other literature streams in organizational research. Chapter 3 is devoted to building the conceptual tools.

Case 2A: Coal Mining

How do changes in activities and outcomes at one level or unit relate to changes in activities and outcomes at another level or unit?

Consider the mining organization (depicted in Figure 2.1) that owns 20 mines. Each mine is divided into production areas called sections. Each section, in turn, is composed of three 8-hour crews, and crews are composed of seven to eight members. I selected this form of organization because I have spent a lot of time in this industry; perhaps more important, there are some nice features of this production setting. The sections in a mine are fairly independent of each other—that is, what one section does has little consequence for others. Also, the outcomes for the crew (tons per hour) are measured in the same way at the section, mine, and corporate level. In many other organizations, one does not find this isomorphic feature about outcomes. The outcomes from one unit typically are combined with another unit to create different outcomes. For example, the outputs of a body shop in an automobile plant are different from the outputs of the assembly unit. It is much easier to trace outcome changes at one unit and/or level to another when the outcomes are the same and the units (e.g., sections) are independent of each other. This is an important observation regarding linkages that is revisited later in the book.

Let's go back to Figure 2.1 and imagine some scenarios. Suppose a training program is introduced to improve miner-level capabilities and there are observable improvements in the miners' individual-level performance, such as when the "bolter" puts more bolts into the ceiling at a faster and safer rate after training. Let's assume we wanted to determine if changes in individual activities were reflected in group-level changes. What would your guess be? One option is that individual-level training improved individual performance and group level performance. Another option is that individual-level performance increased, but not group-level performance. In this setting, interdependence within the group is key. Knowing that the crew members can perform their individual tasks more effectively tells us little about the critical issue—whether performance of the group task will improve (Moreland, 1999). If improvements in individual performance are integrated in the group task, there may be some relation between individual and group output changes. Also, there are a lot of exogenous and unpredictable factors that affect the group's performance. In mining, a

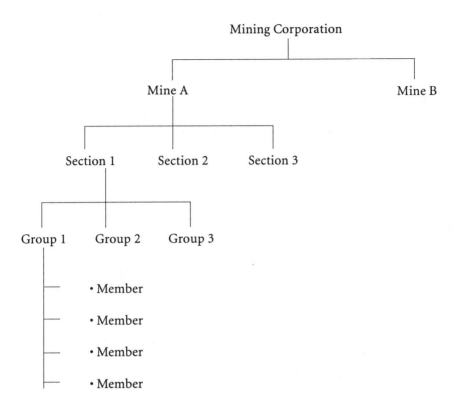

Figure 2.1. Mining Organization

bad roof, lots of water, and machine breakdowns can dominate the work life of such a group, independent of training and improvements in individual-level productivity.

What if a group's performance increases as a function of individual training? Will the changes in group performance be observable at the section level? The answer is not obvious. Although the three groups within a section work at different times, they are interdependent in the following sense. Mining has a series of activities that includes both direct production (i.e., mining) and indirect production (i.e., activities that prepare a section for mining and for meeting safety regulations). These activities do not naturally fall on the 8-hour shift cycle. This means that it is possible for some groups to focus on direct production activities and leave the indirect activities for the next shift. This form of suboptimization leads to conflict among the groups and lowers productivity, that is, individual-level training leads to group-level productivity increases, which, in turn, lead to conflict and an overall decrease in section-level productivity. This observation that improvements in performance at one level or unit may lead to decrements in performance in other units is developed throughout the book, particularly in Chapter 7. One key for better section performance is joint optimization. Whether a change in group-level productivity results in the section-level productivity change depends on the propensity for joint optimization among the three crews, which may or may not be affected by the individual-level training.

Let's assume everything is "working well" and the section performance indicators (productivity and safety) are up. Will performance changes at the section level be reflected in changes at the mine level? On one hand, because there are no interdependencies among the sections, there should be a direct connection between change in the section and changes at the mine level. On the other hand, the mine is a system with other constraints. For example, the coal needs to be moved from the section to a cleaning plant, which is on the surface, before it is shipped to the customer. If the transportation system cannot move the increased amount of coal to the plant, we would not see any changes in the mine-level outcomes. Or if the cleaning plant cannot process the coal for the customer at the rate that is produced by the section, we would not see any mine-level outcome changes in production. This example highlights issues of constraints in interdependent production systems. Strategies related to line balancing or fully integrated manufacturing systems (Fine, 1998) are designed to permit downstream operations to absorb changes in prior production settings.

I could continue this example by asking whether changes in productivity at the mine level would lead to performance changes at the corporate level. Given that the outcomes are the same (i.e., tons of coal/time), I would look for factors that may enhance or inhibit the linkages between mine-level changes and corporate changes. For example, if the contract between the mining corporation and its customers (e.g., utility companies) provided incentives for additional coal production, the increased productivity at the mine should contribute to greater corporate productivity and additional revenues (Chapter 6 discusses this particular linkage in detail).

I presented this example because I want to create images of work and set the linkage concept in these images. What are some ideas that come from this example? First, tracing these changes in the mining example across levels is fairly complicated, even in this simple situation. This situation is labeled "simple" because the outcomes are in the same metric (e.g., tons/hours) across levels, and, at least at the section level, the units are independent.

Second, the similarity of outcomes across levels or units is an important concept in this book that is developed in the next chapter. Identifying the similarities or differences in outcomes is critical to understanding organizational linkages.

Third, the forms of interdependencies (Thompson, 1967) also are critical in understanding linkages. The correlation between changes in individual performance and group performance is influenced by the form of interdependence. In highly interdependent activities such as a mining crew, improvements in individual performance may not lead to improvements in group performance.

Fourth, the sign of the changes at one level or unit may be positive, zero, or negative on another unit or level. In the mining example, high performance of one group in this setting may reduce productivity of the other groups in a given section, and overall productivity may decrease.

Finally, in my portrayal of the mining example, the focus was on the internal part of the organization, the technical system, with a fairly mechanistic perspective. However, we know that in any organizational system there are predictable and unpredictable events that shape the organization's activities, we know that there is both order and chaos (Gleick, 1987), and we know that there are multiple subsystems (e.g., technical, social) at play (Katz & Kahn, 1966). We know in this organizational setting and others that there are many exogenous, unpredictable shocks to the system (e.g., changes in physical conditions) that send reverberations, sometimes chaotic in nature, throughout the system. In some cases, there are known or understandable ways to respond to these unexpected shocks, and, in other cases, there are not. The unpredictable shocks are not always about the technological subsystem. For instance, a change in union leadership leads to a grievance that explodes into a major labor/management conflict that becomes manifested in a slowdown of production across the organization. The controversy is not predictable; the manifestation in lower productivity is understandable but difficult to respond to and change.

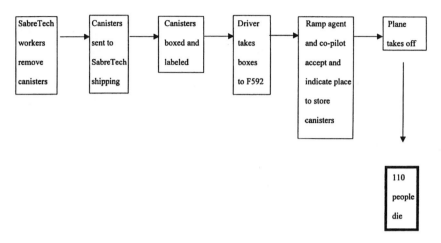

Figure 2.2. Activities, Events, and Outcomes for Flight 592

Case 2B: ValuJet

Let's look at a different sequence of events to provide a contrast to Figure 2.1. In Figure 2.2, I show an account of some of the critical events in the ValuJet Flight 592 disaster. One hundred and ten persons died when the plane crashed in the Florida Everglades in 1996. I will not provide a detailed analysis of the causes of this accident here (see Chapter 4, Organizational Errors). I selected this case because of its contrast with the mining example. In that example, we were tracing *vertical* changes in outcomes, that is, we followed outcome changes at the individual level to outcome changes at the group, section, mine, and corporate levels. In this exploration of ValuJet, the focus is on *horizontal changes,* that is, we follow changes among horizontal units that eventually affect organizational-level outcomes.

ValuJet, a 2-year-old airline, hired SabreTech, a maintenance organization, to recondition its MD-80 airplanes. These planes were to join the ValuJet fleet. Removing oxygen canisters was one of many activities. The workers apparently removed the canisters from the plane, failed to put safety caps over the firing pins, and stacked the canisters in cardboard boxes. There were clear rules about putting safety caps on the firing pins. Some time (in weeks) elapsed before the boxes were moved to shipping. The boxes remained in shipping until a manager requested that the area be cleaned up. The boxes were sealed, labeled as aircraft parts, and eventually delivered to Flight 592. ValuJet was prohibited from carrying hazardous material—the materials were hazardous. The ramp attendant accepted the material. Also, the copilot, the last point of control, accepted the material that was placed in the forward hold. Chemical reactions in these canisters were capable of creating high levels of heat and fire. Fire from the canisters was a primary cause for the crash.

At one level, this is a similar story to the mining example. We have a series of activities and outcomes. In the mining case, we started with changes in individual outcomes (i.e., productivity). The outcomes in this case are errors defined as deviations (e.g., mechanics did not put on safety caps) from written organizational expectations and regulations. The task is to trace through the series of activities and outcomes to understand how the individual errors accumulated until an organizational error occurred in the tragedy of Flight 592.

In ValuJet, the setting is different. I did not draw a multilevel organizational hierarchy as in the mining case (see Figure 2.1). Here, we have a set of horizontal or sequential events (e.g., mechanics removing the canisters, the copilot indicating where to store the canisters) that seem related to the final tragedy. Also, there are two different organizations working together, as portrayed by the outsource organization, SabreTech, and the principal, ValuJet.

The outcomes in this example are different across levels. For the worker removing the oxygen canisters, the metrics are the number and perhaps quality of jobs done. For the organization, it is the loss of life, reputation, financial costs, and ultimate survival. Forms of organizing play a role here, but in a different manner. In the mining case, the interdependencies were largely technological. There was very tight coupling among crew members within the sections and relative independence between work sections. In ValuJet, interdependence is largely interorganizational between a vendor and a customer. This form of the interdependence is relatively loose. SabreTech agreed to recondition some planes for ValuJet by a certain deadline. But the sequence of events in Figure 2.2 is not closely tied to the production system of ValuJet, which moves people between assigned locations, or, for that matter, of SabreTech.

The most outstanding difference between the two cases probably is the connectivity of events in terms of time. In the mining case, if a crew stopped production because of mechanical failure, there would be a direct, predictable impact on the mine's production. There was no predictable sequence between the maintenance work by SabreTech and the crash of Flight 592. The canisters sat in the mechanics' area for some time. There was no clear reason why they were moved. Again, they sat in the shipping area until a manager came by and asked the area to be cleaned up because a prospective customer was to visit the area. There is no connection, temporally or otherwise, between this manager's intervention and Flight 592. Finally, the movement of the canister from shipping to Flight 592 was not preprogrammed. The availability of a driver, which was conditioned on other factors, created a connection with this flight. If the driver was available earlier or later, it might have been another flight going to Atlanta. If it was a different flight, it is hard to predict the final outcomes. This cargo was not identified as hazardous, but a new flight brings a new ramp attendant, a new copilot, perhaps a different plane, and different configurations of cargo. Each of these factors might have prevented the canisters from going on board. Or, even if they were on board, whatever conditions triggered the canisters might have not occurred. The images about time and causation are pretty loose. The events seem to unfold. One key trigger—the request by the manager to clean up the area—seems quite independent of activities of removing and disposing of the canisters. The connection between the shipping department and the plane seems pretty loose and random. In the end, the movement of the canisters was determined by the availability of the driver and a plane that was going to Atlanta.

Making Sense of Exceptions

I close this particular story by focusing on "chains of meanings." As social scientists or as actors in everyday life, we have a natural tendency to create meaning out of chains of events. Fortunately or unfortunately, we like to focus on making sense of the exception rather than of the routine. We tend to work backward from some outcome and build chains of meaning in explaining this outcome to ourselves as well as others (Weick, 1995). In the case of the ValuJet story, we try to identify events and arrange them in some sensible, temporal order prior to the crash. The events were from shipping to the ramp agent and copilot, and then to the plane, not in the opposite order. But we do more than identify, describe, and order. We assign meaning to sequences of events. One form of meaning deals with causality regarding the sequence of events. Think about my description of ValuJet. There is a decline in information about the objects to be put on the plane prior to its takeoff as we arrange the sequence of events. The maintenance people and their supervisors had more information than the ramp attendant. By the time the shipping person received the carton with the canisters, it was labeled as "repairable." The boxes with the canisters were relabeled "aircraft parts." One explanation is that the decline in information reduced the vigilance of the ramp attendant and the copilot. The request by the manager to clean up the area helps create meaningful links between the canisters and the plane. But, we can tell only part of the story. In some accounts of the crash, it is asserted that the safety caps were not available. Why were the safety caps not available? What is the chain of events that explains that phenomenon? Why did canisters ignite? Was it during loading or movement of the cargo during takeoff?

My points are (a) there are many missing chains of explanation, and (b) there is indeterminacy among these events or chains. We cannot and should not be able to tell complete stories. Diane Vaughan's (1996) book on the Challenger disaster is a case in point. It is the most detailed rich account of organizational activities I have ever read. It is more than just the detail that captures the reader. There is an organizational detective at work uncovering and providing meaning to a complicated set of events embedded in a very complex system. But even in this book, which is an exemplar of organizational research, there still are missing links and unexplained connections. Was it a wind shear plus cold weather that interacted with other elements in the launch to cause this disaster? We will never know and may have never been able to know.

I want you to reflect on these two stories as we develop the conceptual tools for linkage analysis. These two concrete sets of images sharpen some of the concepts, such as outcome metric similarity and forms of organizing, that are developed in Chapter 3. Indeed, in telling the stories of the mining case and ValuJet, I have tried to delineate some of the basic tools of linkage analysis.

Concluding Thoughts

- Organizational linkages refer to the connections among activities and outcomes across units and/or levels.
- The basic question remains the same: How are changes in activities and outcomes at one unit or level related to changes in activities and outcomes at another level?
- Organizational linkages appear in different forms of organizing. The mining organization lends itself more to vertical linkages, ValuJet more to horizontal linkages across different organizations.
- The concept of outcome similarity seems important in the task of tracing changes across levels. In the mining example, one principal outcome variable— tons/hours—is common across most units such as the group, section, and mine. This should make it easier to trace changes across levels. On the other hand, the outcomes in the units in the ValuJet case are different across units and levels.
- The concept of interdependence appears in many ways with respect to:
  — Location—among team members, between groups
  — Degree—tight or loose coupling
  — Content—technological, organizational, social
  — Temporal dimensions—short to long time delays

  All these elements set the foundation in framing the linkage problem.

- In our subsequent analysis of organizational linkages, we expect to find both predictable and unpredictable connections among activities and outcomes across levels. Predictability is reflected in how changes in crew activities and outcomes can affect section level outcomes directly. Unpredictability is manifested in the connections between removing the canisters, their delivery to Flight 592, and the subsequent disaster. Also, we find ourselves in settings combining order with disorder.
- Linkage analysis can be applied to different forms of organizing, but the form of organizing (e.g., the mining organization vs. ValuJet) will shape the linkage analysis.
- Our effort to build chains of meaning in linkage analysis is challenged by missing chains and levels of indeterminancy.

Conversation Two

You: I like the examples, but I am not sure that organizational linkages is that new of a concept.

PSG: My position is that the linkage concept is a new perspective in organizational analysis, but manifestation of it can be discerned in a variety of literatures. There is not a nice cumulative body of research on organizational linkages. There are, however, ties to research on topics such as levels (Roberts et al., 1978), interdependence (Thompson, 1967), dynamic systems (Sterman, 1994), and chaos theory (Gleick, 1987). Perhaps you can cite some research that you think is the same as linkage analysis but has a different name.

You: The literature on groups has moved to a multilevel perspective. Let me give you one of many possible examples. There is research on individual and group goals (Crown & Rosse, 1995) that basically shows that the compatibility of individual team member goals and group goals are important predictors in understanding group performance, particularly in interdependent tasks. That sounds like your mining example, in which training individuals to improve their productivity may or may not have any impact on group-level productivity.

PSG: I like your example. The similarities with my example of the mining case are fairly straightforward in terms of a focus on multiple levels and the importance of task interdependencies. Let me focus on the difference versus the similarities.

First, the study you cited, as well as others (Hollenbeck et al., 1998), are about understanding group effectiveness. The specific studies do an excellent job in theoretically and empirically showing that a multilevel perspective increases our understanding of different measures of group effectiveness. Organizational linkage analysis asks a different question: If groups are more effective because of goal compatibility (Crown & Rosse, 1995) or better feedback systems (Hollenbeck et al., 1998), how will these changes in group outcomes affect other levels of analysis? Using the mining case, if group performance increases as a function of goal compatibility, what are the implications of these observed changes on other levels of analysis, such as the section, mine, or corporation? Organizational linkage analysis would start with a state of increased group effectiveness and ask how that new level of effectiveness would affect other units.

A second difference is that organizational linkage analysis needs to be applied in a variety of organizational settings. In the two studies we discussed, the group setting was characterized by highly interdependent tasks. We want to look at different forms of groups in different organizational settings. I introduced the ValuJet example because it represents a different form of organizing. It can help us to understand organizational linkages by examining different forms of organizations.

Finally, another way I think about linkages is that it focuses on untested organizational assumptions. I mentioned that most of the research I have done on groups assumes that improvement in group-level performance leads to improvements at the individual and organizational level. This assumption, particularly about organizational level changes, is rarely tested. Later, in Chapter 6, we examine system-level changes that demonstrate positive organizational-level outcomes. Within this particular research tradition, there are clear assumptions that these system-level changes create individual-level and group-level changes that are compatible to the organizational outcomes. But these assumptions are not examined or tested. Organizational linkage analysis focuses on these assumptions.

You: Let me give you one other example. There is a set of papers by Kozlowski, Salas and others (cf. Kozlowski & Salas, 1997) that presents a multilevel organizational systems approach for the implementation and transfer of training. The integrative framework by Kozlowski and Salas (p. 10) clearly focuses on the linkages among individuals, units, and organizational levels. Does their system-based model not pick up the essence of the organizational linkages concept?

PSG: That particular model and stream of research is important because it conceptualizes training in a multilevel perspective. There is a strong focus on context and on the congruency between context factors, such as form of interdependence, technology, culture, and training. This congruence within and across levels affects the effectiveness of transfer of training.

The basic differences between the linkage perspective and this integrative model of training are (a) we are primarily interested in the results of training on performance and examining the impact of changes in performance at one level (e.g., unit) on another (e.g., individual or organization), and (b) the conditions when changes at one level will or will not affect changes in activities and outcomes at another unit or level. Training as articulated in this integrative model may play a part in understanding one of the conditions when changes at one level may affect another. There are obviously many other human resource strategies (e.g., pay, participation) that should be considered as well. In addition, there are other organizational features, such as the similarity of outcomes across units and the form of organizing, that need to be integrated in any linkage analysis.

Let's move to a more formal consideration of the organizational linkage concept as a way to sharpen similarities and differences with other concepts.

3 Tools for Linkage Analysis

This chapter begins our exploration of tools for organizational linkage analysis. When we think about the Barings bankruptcy, the productivity paradox, impacts of training in the mining example, or ValuJet, we need some tools for analysis. Table 3.1 identifies the major tools for organizational linkage analysis. This chapter explores (a) outcome coupling and (b) positive and negative feedback systems as analytic tools for understanding why changes in activities and outcomes in some unit or level affect activities and outcomes at another level. Other concepts of (a) limiting conditions and (b) compensatory process mechanisms are only listed here and then explored in detail in Chapters 5 and 6, respectively. My goal is to show the reader a quick snapshot of the basic tools in the linkage tool box.

As we move through this book together, I delineate each tool and its components and then apply the tool to enhance our understanding of the central linkage question. As a new tool is introduced, I specify its relations to the existing set of tools in the context of analyzing linkages questions. In Chapters 6 to 8, I illustrate the use of all the tools and the order in which they may be used most appropriately.

This chapter begins with a definition of organizational linkages. Then, I develop the conceptual tools of outcome coupling and feedback systems. It closes with a discussion about context. Because organizational linkage analysis focuses on real organizations, one of the first tasks is to define the social system for analysis. This refers to which aspect of the organization (e.g., people, activities, units, and system outcomes) we should examine. In the ValuJet example, one could look at the ValuJet organization alone, or also SabreTech, the maintenance

Table 3.1   Major Tools for Organizational Linkage Analysis

Type	Tool	Function
1	Outcome coupling	To identify structural properties (e.g., outcome metric similarity) that may facilitate (or inhibit) changes in activities and outcomes in one unit or level from affecting changes in activities or outcomes in another unit or level
2	Negative and positive feedback systems	General mechanisms that explain why changes in activities and outcomes at one level will (or will not) affect changes in activities and outcomes at a different unit or level
3	Limiting conditions	To identify organizational situations (e.g., constraints) in which positive changes in activities and outcomes at one unit or level will not affect changes in activities and outcomes at another unit or level
4	Compensatory process mechanisms	Specific organizational processes (e.g., reactive problem solving, focus of attention) that explain why changes in activities and outcomes at one level or unit will affect changes in activities and outcomes at a different unit or level

organization, and/or the FAA. What is the appropriate time period to consider when analyzing ValuJet—at the time of the crash, at the time of outsourcing the work to SabreTech, or when ValuJet began operations? Defining the social system for analysis, both in terms of critical actors and time, makes a difference.

Defining Organizational Linkages

Organizational linkages refer to the connections between activities, events, and outcomes. In the dictionary, the word *link* or *linkages* refers to connecting objects. The objects in this context can be activities (i.e., things that people do). In the coal mining case, a miner cuts coal from the face, a mechanic repairs a machine, or a utility person conducts safety activities such as rock dusting to prevent explosions. In the ValuJet case, the maintenance person removed the oxygen canisters, the shipping clerk labeled the canisters "aircraft parts," and the driver delivered the canisters to Flight 592. Activities are definable units of work produced by an individual.

Another linked object is an event. Events are cycles or groups of interrelated activities that represent some unit of work. In production settings, cycles or groups of activities are fairly defined. If you visit your post office's production facility, you will see a large automated factory. Within the factory are classes of machines such as multiline optical character readers that read printed addresses and print bar codes. There is a clear cycle of activities, including feeding and sweeping that machine and moving the mail. These interrelated sets of activities are produced by two or more people. In the mining case, there is a clear cycle of activities involved in cutting coal and then transporting it to a belt. There are other cycles of interrelated activities, such as preparing an area for mining. In the ValuJet case, we can distinguish a specific activity, such as removing the canister from the airplane being renovated, to a cycle of activities that includes removing the canister, placing the safety cap on the open valve, labeling the canister as hazardous material, storing the canister, and obtaining a "sign off" of this work by the supervisor. Sometimes we need to look at an activity, and sometimes it is more convenient to talk about bundles or cycles of interrelated activities.

The other object is an outcome. An outcome refers to the output of a system and can be thought of as effectiveness indicators (Cameron & Whetten, 1983; Meyer & Gupta, 1994). I have used outcome terminology such as productivity, bankruptcy (Barings), physical disaster (Challenger), and reputation loss (SabreTech). Customer satisfaction, quality, adaptability, and morale are also outcome indicators. These indicators appear within different units of analysis (individual, dyad, group, department, etc.). The metrics of these outcomes may or may not be isomorphic across levels. In the mining example, tons per hour works at all relevant levels of analysis (crew, section, mine, corporation). In contrast, in an automobile factory the body shop output is not measured using the same metrics as the assembly group. Likewise, the output of a product development group is different from the output of a manufacturing group.

Table 3.2 presents the basic terminology used in this book. The terms *level* and *unit* also are defined. To clarify the relation between the three linked objects (activities, events, and outcomes), recall the Barings case. In that case, there were individual activities such as trades and set-

Table 3.2 Basic Terms

Term	Definition	Examples
Activity	Definable unit of work produced by an individual	• Removing the canisters • Labeling the canisters aircraft parts
Event	Cycle of interrelated activities performed by two or more people	• Initiating, settling, and recording a trade
Outcome	Output of some production system	• Coal tons/day • Customer satisfaction
Level	A hierarchical location in organizational space	• Individual • Group • Organizational
Unit	An organizational subsystem that produces some goods or services	• Design unit • Customer service unit • Production unit

tlements as well as cycles of trades and settlements defined by reporting procedures. Other events included creating an internal report, presenting the report, and monitoring trading activities. A variety of outcomes appeared at different levels of the organization—bankruptcy, loss of reputation, jail time for the trader, and loss of employment. These activities, events, and outcomes were being played out in the Singapore office, the London headquarters of the bank, the regulatory bodies in England and Singapore, the media, and so on. Organizational linkages focus on the connections among these activities, events, and outcomes through this extended social system and over time. Our goal is to understand how structural and dynamic properties that facilitate or inhibit changes in activities, events, and outcomes at one level or unit affect changes in activities, events, and outcomes at another level or unit.

Figure 3.1 illustrates one possible scenario between activities and outcomes at one level with other levels and over time. I have left out

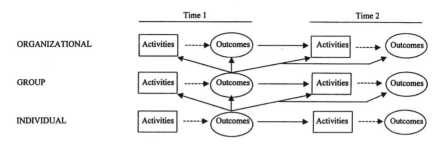

Figure 3.1. Organizational Linkages

events to simplify the diagram. This figure presents a bottom-up linkage from individual to group to organization and horizontal and vertical connections over time. Individual-level activities lead to individual
outcomes, which, in turn, can affect group-level activities and outcomes at $time_1$. These changes in individual and group activities and
outcomes at $time_1$ can affect individual and group activities at $time_2$, as
well as organizational-level activities and outcomes. The figure is
meant to be illustrative, not exhaustive. There are many other possible
connections in this figure. Also, I could have presented a top-down figure that would have illustrated how changes in outcomes at the organizational level (e.g., declining profits) may have had impacts on group
and individual activities and outcomes both at $time_1$ and $time_2$. The basic idea is to develop some simple visual representations of organizational linkages. Many other scenarios or combinations are possible.

Understanding Figure 3.1 in a particular organizational context is the
essence of understanding organizational linkages. What is missing is the
nature of these linkages or connections. Let's turn to some other tools
that will help us to build our understanding of organizational linkages.

Outcome Coupling

Outcome coupling refers to the dimensions of the outcomes in different
units or levels. There are three I want to explore.

First, are the *metrics* the same or different? In the Barings example,
the outcomes for the Singapore office and the parent company are the

same—British pounds and profits. In the ValuJet case, the outcomes are different across units. The quality indicators in the outsourced maintenance group are different from the outcomes following the crash of Flight 592. The basic principle is that it is easier to trace changes in outcomes that are similar. A $500,000 increase in profits from the Barings office in Singapore should be directly traceable to variations in profits in Barings. However, the connection between an increase in the number of new product designs at Allied Manufacturing and profitability at the plant level is more difficult to trace. Common metrics make it easier to trace changes across levels but do not address the nature of the connections across levels or units.

The second dimension of outcome coupling is the *forms of organizing*. What are the forms of organizing in which outcomes are embedded? I use Thompson's (1967) distinction among additive, sequential, and reciprocal forms of interdependence, a well-known typology that is generalizable to different units of analysis (e.g., organizations, groups).

An *additive* form is composed of a series of independent units, each producing goods and services independent of the other. In the mining example, there is no connection between the changes in Section A's activities, events, and outcomes and Section B's activities, events, and outcomes. The additive form outcomes combine independently to create the total outcomes of the principal unit. In some additive organizations, there may be common financial or coordinating features in terms of advertising services provided by the principal unit, but it is not a critical feature.

Sequential forms, by definition, have interdependence across units. In an automobile assembly plant, there are three main units—a body shop, a paint shop, and an assembly area. There is only one sequence across these units. The body is welded, typically by a very creative team of robots. Then the body is painted by another, more artistic group of robots. (There are some parallels between watching a robotic paint shop and a string quartet.) Finally, the auto is assembled with all of its component parts. These sequential arrangements are important. Using technology to increase productivity in the body shop may or may not have any impact on the total plant. Increases in productivity in the body shop need to be matched by the capabilities of other units in the sequence to capitalize on the increases, which, in turn, would affect plant productivity.

Reciprocal forms of interdependence have multiple units interacting together in different combinations on different objects. Multiple units of a bank may serve the same corporation in different ways. Providing lines of credit, trading on behalf of the customer, and servicing international operations represent distinct independent operations. However, when focused on the same customer, changing lines of credit may lead to changes in trading limits. Results of trading behavior may affect lines of credit, and so on.

Why present these organizational forms, and how do they help in organizational linkage analysis? They represent a way to describe connections between levels or units in which outcomes are embedded. If I know the units are additive, I can expect changes in activities and outcomes at one level to affect changes in another level directly. When we analyze the Barings case in the next chapter, we see that a key trading unit had an additive relation to the parent organization. To me, that means that changes in profit or loss from the unit are directly tied to profit and loss changes in the parent company. On the other hand, if the product design group in Allied Manufacturing increased the number of new product designs, I know these designs need to go through a complicated sequential set of transformations (e.g., converting designs to manufacturing processes, manufacturing the product, distribution, and sales) before we would observe any changes in the plant's profitability. And I know that understanding the connection between improved designs and profitability will be a difficult task. This example entails a very complicated set of causal paths. Reciprocal forms represent a more complicated way of organizing, and, therefore, the changes in one unit on another are much more difficult to ascertain.

The third dimension is the *nature of the connections,* given any form of organizing. Consider an automobile assembly plant—a sequential form of organizing. For illustrative purposes, let's assume we introduced vision technology (which provides 100% inspection of all parts) in the first main operation—the body shop—to improve the quality of the whole plant. I would want to ask three questions about the nature of the connections:

- How many *connections* or *intermediary activities* or *events* occur between the body shop and the completion of the final product—the assembled car? There are likely to be hundreds of activities, given the complexity of current vehicles. The greater the number of intermediary activities, the more likely that attenuating factors (e.g., coordination costs) or random events will reduce the impact of improvements of quality in the body shop on plant-level quality.

- To what extent are the connections between these intermediary activities *programmed* or *unprogrammed*? In an automobile assembly plant, the activities are a highly programmed sequence of operations. There is a fixed set of relations among activities in the body shop that precede those in the paint shop. In other types of work domains (e.g., architecture, a trading house), the interrelations between intermediary activities or events are much less programmed. The more programmed the activities, the more likely coordination problems and constraints may mitigate the impact of changes at one level affecting another.

- What is the *temporal* relation between changes in activities and outcomes at one level and corresponding changes at another level? Do changes in outcomes at one level instantaneously affect activities, events, and outcomes at another level, or are there long lead times? In many auto assembly plants, 60 to 70 vehicles are being produced each hour. Any vehicle's life in the plant is quite short. Therefore, the time lags between changes in activities and outcomes in one unit on another are likely to be quite short. The shorter the time lag, the easier it will be to trace changes in one unit or level on another.

The discussion of these three features—the number of intermediary activities or events, the extent to which they are programmed, and the time lags among these activities—were in terms of a sequential form of interdependence. These features also would fit other forms of organizing. Consider the coal mining case, an additive form of organization. Even in that case, there are intermediary activities between each unit and the organization. The coal needs to be transported from the section or unit to the cleaning plant and then transported to the customer. In this example, we can determine the number of intermediate activities, the extent to which they are programmed, and the time lags between producing coal in the sections to the delivery of coal to the customer.

Figure 3.2 summarizes the discussion about outcome coupling. I am proposing a multidimensional continuum, which characterizes the structural properties associated with the form of linkages between units or levels. At one extreme, we have an organization with common metrics for outcomes and that is organized in an additive form. There are few intermediate activities between outcomes at one level or unit and another. They are not programmed together, and there are short lags between changes in activities and outcomes across levels or units. In the chart we are beginning to build, the causal paths are simpler and

METRICS	Same ↔ Different
FORMS OF ORGANIZING	Additive ↔ Sequential ↔ Reciprocal
NATURE OF CONNECTIONS	
Number	Few ↔ Many
Programmed	Low ↔ High
Time Lags	Short ↔ Long

Figure 3.2. Dimensions of Outcome Coupling

more direct, and the timing of changes from one level to another is more immediate. Here, we are better able to trace how changes in activities at one level or unit affect other levels or units. As we shift to different metrics or to a large number of intermediary activities with longer delays, it is going to be more difficult to trace and understand changes in outcomes across levels or units.

I recommend the use of the outcome coupling tool to begin any organizational linkage analysis. The three dimensions (Figure 3.2) and related questions provide an initial way to map the structural properties of the linkages. This mapping is not purely descriptive. Within each of the dimensions, there are specific *ex ante* propositions regarding how to trace out changes across levels or units.

Another part of linkage analysis is identification of mechanisms that explain why changes at one level or unit impact another level or unit, that is, given the initial mapping along the outcome coupling dimensions in Figure 3.1, what are some of the mechanisms or dynamic processes that can facilitate or inhibit changes across levels or units?

Negative Feedback Systems

Feedback systems provide an important process component of any dynamic system. They play an important theoretical role in several streams of literature, such as Weick's (1979) work on organizing, the system dynamics (Sterman, 1994), and research on organizational change (Argyris, 1985, 1990; Nadler et al., 1992; Nadler et al., 1995). We consider both negative and positive feedback systems. These two systems have properties that should help our linkage analysis.

In a negative feedback system, there is an organizational entity, a desired state, and an actual state. The discrepancy between the desired state and the actual state typically leads to change in the organization. The change moves the system to a state of equilibrium in which the desired and actual states are equivalent. In our subsequent analysis of organizational errors, we look at deviations from expected or desired practices (i.e., the actual state vs. the desired state). For example, what happens when a trader in Barings exceeds daily trading limits? What are the organizational systems and practices that identify the deviation between desired and actual practices and initiate changes to return the system to some equilibrium period? Analyzing these systems and processes in terms of whether they work can provide some insights into how events at one level (e.g., individual trader errors) can affect organizational level outcomes.

In our analysis of organizational change (Chapters 5-7), negative feedback loops can play a useful role. Any major organizational change is really a series of changes. The existence of feedback and redesign mechanisms is a critical part of any change process (Goodman, 1982). Consider the earlier example in which self-designed teams were introduced in a factory. This complicated series of changes affected authority, communication, decision making, and reward subsystems. In a large intervention like this, there are bound to be discrepancies between desired activities and actual activities. For example, a pay-for-knowledge system is not working, or the supervisors are unwilling to let the team make more decisions. In either of these instances, negative feedback loops identify discrepancies between actual and desired states and initiate changes to bring the desired and actual behaviors in line.

Although the concept of a negative feedback system seems quite straightforward, it has a number of interesting implications for our linkage analysis. First, the gap may occur between actual and desired states, but it is not measured. Without measurement, in this case, there would be no initiative to change the system, and the organizational entity may deteriorate over time. Second, the gap may be measured and known to relevant actors, but still no action follows. In the Barings case, there were trading limits that were exceeded and measured, but still no action occurred. Eventually, there were dire consequences. Third, the gap may be known, but there is a delay in initiating changes to bring the actual and desired state into line, in which case the effects of the change are reduced. The issue then is to understand and assess the impact of delays in organizational outcomes. Some studies (Diehl & Sterman, 1995) have shown that the length of delays in responding significantly affects the rate of performance declines.

To use negative feedback systems as a means to provide insights on tracing how activities, events, and outcomes at one level may affect other levels, consider the following questions. Are desired behaviors or expectations clearly stated and understood? What monitoring systems, if any, are in place? The absence of a monitoring system is an important part of the story in the ValuJet case. Another question to ask is whether the organizations respond to gaps between actual and desired behaviors. Are there delays in responding either to adjust the system to its desired state or to adjust its desired state to actual conditions? How do these delays affect the system and performance outcomes?

Positive Feedback Systems

In positive feedback systems, there is no equilibrium (Sterman, 1994; Weick, 1979). Changes in one entity lead to changes in another, which accelerate changes in the first entity, and so on. The organization is continually moving in a direction rather than seeking some equilibrium. In these feedback systems, small initial changes may have amplified effects over time. There also is some level of instability in these systems to consider.

An interesting body of research by Sterman et al. (1997) illustrates the positive feedback loop phenomena. They examined total quality management (TQM) change efforts through a system dynamics perspective, which includes positive and negative loops. To discuss the relation between commitment and defects, let's start with a simple example. TQM change efforts usually start with a push from top management, which captures the commitment and energy of a few people in early pilot projects. If the initial projects are successful, the visibility of early results may increase the number (say, 10%) of committed workers independent of the push from management. More committed workers create more successful projects, which leads to the commitment of more workers. A positive acceleration cycle is under way. Initially, it was fueled by the push from management.

Now, the results plus the increasing number of committed people are energizing the system. And the changes are not linear. The change from 30% to 40% committed workers will have a greater impact on increasing the number of committed workers than the change from 0% to 10% committed workers.

Eventually, this positively accelerating cycle is going to slow down for at least two reasons. First, eventually, the number of workers will approach 100%, and the force of committed workers motivating uncommitted workers will drop. Also, the defect rate is likely to move to some minimum. Therefore, positive results are harder to come by, and this motivator declines. At this point, the system may remain the same or begin to cycle slowly, and then more rapidly, in the opposite direction. What will transpire will depend on the following: The initial level of commitment probably will offset any initial downward cycle (Sproull & Hofmeister, 1986). In most TQM change efforts, people focus on the more routine operations in which it is easier to find and demonstrate quality improvements (Dean & Goodman, 1993). As one applies TQM principles to less routine operations, it is likely to take longer, and it may be more difficult to demonstrate results. This delay in demonstrating results is very difficult to predict. The consequence is that people may pull out of these projects too early, which is an acknowledgment of failure. This, in turn, can lead to lower levels of resources and management support in other projects, which, in turn, lead to lower commitment, which, in turn, affects lower performance and fewer resources. The negative cycle has begun.

I introduced this example to give a verbal picture of positive feedback loops. Let's try to pull from this example some concepts that will help us understand linkages. One concept is *initial conditions* (Gleick, 1987). The basic idea is that small initial changes might become amplified over time. We need to see if this concept will help us to reveal some of the linkages between outcomes at one level and those of another.

Another key idea in the TQM example is *accelerating cycles.* Once these cycles begin, they pick up speed and accelerate. They can move in positive or negative directions. Also, the changes are somewhat unstable. A number of things seem to be driving the acceleration. The impact of rates of change in one system on another may be related to the point of change. For example, the change from 0% to 10% of the people committed to TQM efforts probably has a lower impact than a change of 30% to 40% of the people committed. The latter 10% change creates more visibility and legitimation for the change effort and a relatively greater force on the uncommitted to join. Another factor affecting the acceleration is the introduction of other systems that are synergistic with the existing systems. For example, my original example included management push, commitment, and quality improvement. Let's assume the initial success attracts more resources in the form of more training and expert support. This resource variable should interact with the other variables to speed up the acceleration process, which, in turn, might lead to access to more resources. As the positive acceleration process builds in this organizational change example, we should expect to observe changes in activities and outcomes at the individual or group levels producing more direct impact on changes in outcomes at the organizational level.

A third concept implicit in this example is *time*. The question is, when does the acceleration cycle kick off? We also could ask when will it slow down or reverse itself? For illustration purposes, let's go back to management's introduction of TQM. There is an initial push for TQM, resulting in some pilot projects. Let's assume these pilots will be successful. However, that does not happen instantly. People need to be trained and to learn how to work effectively in teams. There are likely to be false starts and other delays. This means that there are time lags between the push for TQM and results. Also, initial results may attract a few others to the TQM program, but, as we pointed out, increasing the number of committed personnel from 0% to 5% will not have much of an effect on reducing defects, which, in turn, will not affect the rate of committed workers.

The implication of this example is that there may be considerable delays before the accelerating process kicks off. Changes are going on, but they are not at a level to initiate the accelerating processes. Unfortunately, we do not have any developed theory to explain this phenomenon. Sterman et al. (1997) did some interesting simulations to model these delays. From other research (McGrath, 1984; Sitkin, Sutcliffe, & Schroeder, 1994), we know the work tasks will make a difference. In more routine work, there may be more opportunities both to build an effective intervention and to measure results of quality improvement programs. In this setting, the delay between introduction of change and the acceleration process may be shorter than in a more nonroutine operation, such as development or strategic planning.

Figure 3.3 provides a summary of the major feedback system dimensions I use subsequently in an analysis of organizational linkages. One can frame each dimension as a question in a linkage analysis. For example, in the analysis of the Barings case in the next chapter, we want to ask whether desired behaviors or activities are explicitly stated, whether monitoring systems exist, whether the organization responds to gaps, and so on. Or we can ask whether there are likely to be relevant initial conditions, whether there are accelerating cycles, their direction, and the timing of these cycles.

Defining the Context

Before one can apply the tools of outcome coupling or negative and positive feedback systems, it is necessary to define the social system for analysis. I see defining the social system or space as a beginning step in a linkage analysis. It is much like building a chart for navigation. We want to identify the spatial and temporal space. You will see this is done in a very iterative way with many boundaries initially undefined. What is the relevant organizational space? What are the relevant unit-unit or unit-organization-relations? Who are the critical actors? On whose activities, events, and outcomes should I focus? What is the relevant time period for identifying the social system?

Consider the case about Allied Manufacturing in which the self-designing teams were successfully implemented, the team performance indicators improved, and no organizational performance outcomes were observed. I am the analyst who wants to tackle this problem. What are the relevant units of analysis—the factory? What about the union members and institutions, both inside and outside the factories? From other research (Zager & Rosow, 1982), we know that changes in international union leadership, although independent from a particular factory or company, can significantly change the functioning of that factory or organization. Is the union at the local, regional, and international level part of the analysis?

Let's go back to ValuJet. If I said we should look at the activities, events, and outcomes within Flight 592, you would indicate that is not an appropriate unit of analysis. I might concede and define the inter-

NEGATIVE LOOPS	
Desired Behavior	Not Stated ↔ Stated
Monitoring Systems	Absent ↔ Present
Organizational Response to Gaps	None ↔ Delayed ↔ Immediate

POSITIVE LOOPS	
Initial Conditions	Absent ↔ Present
Form of Accelerating Cycle	Positive ↔ Negative Direction
	Linear ↔ Nonlinear
Timing of Cycle	Delayed ↔ Immediate

Figure 3.3. Dimensions of Feedback Systems

section between SabreTech and ValuJet as the unit of analysis. Where does the FAA or the National Safety Transportation Board fit in? The FAA had a special team investigating safety incidents of ValuJet before the accident occurred. Why should we include SabreTech as part of the relevant social system? You naturally would point to the canisters as the source of that tragedy. But we really do not know if that is true. Perhaps there were some unobserved problems with the plane that interacted with the canisters. Should we include the maintenance people who serviced the plane or the manufacturer? There are other examples of organizational errors in which the sources of errors are less obvious.

The last example is the most complicated—the Challenger disaster (Vaughan, 1996). Let's look at some quick snapshots. There were meetings the night before the fatal launch. There was a three-way teleconference among managers and engineers, Thiokol (the contractor), the Marshall Space Center, and the Kennedy Space Center. A second conference call occurred several hours later with the same organizations (although some of the players were different). The second conference call was punctuated with an off-line caucus among Thiokol personnel, and then all the players returned. In these meetings, there was a recommendation not to launch, which later was reversed. Another snapshot is of the launch organization for Challenger. This is a very complicated picture, with tens of thousands of people located around the world, myriad contractors, multiple space centers (Johnson, Kennedy), NASA and other governmental organizations, and so on. Or, I might show you series of photos showing you all the review meetings of the first shuttle flight (STS-1) in 1977 through the last review meeting in January 1986 prior to the Challenger launch. The principal players would be people from Thiokol and the Marshall Space Center responsible for the solid rocket booster. I also could show you the elaborate hierarchical review meetings between NASA and its contractors.

What's behind this collage of photos or series of activities is a very significant dilemma. On one hand, to do an analysis of organizational linkages, you need to define the appropriate social system both in terms of actors and time. On the other hand, it is not obvious how to define the appropriate unit of analysis, and different units of analysis generate different linkage analyses. The social system focuses your analysis on a segment of organizational life. The problem is that these analyses become very complex right away, and it is not obvious that the selected unit is the right unit.

Critical Actors

I have some rules of thumb for defining organizational space and the relevant actors. Think about this task as a process in chart making. Charts are necessary for navigation. Creating them is an iterative process. We start off with some boundaries. The boundaries are not fixed and will change. The boundaries are flexible and permeable. In some places, there are no boundaries. In others, the boundaries will be more differentiated over time. There may be some markers (navigational aids) to provide general, but not specific, direction.

First, there is an accumulation of knowledge in the organization literature that should help in defining markers and boundaries. I provide only a few examples. The organizational change literature provides guidance in identifying critical actors (Ault, Walton, & Childers, 1998; Lawler, 1986, 1992; Walton, 1987). For example, in some of the early work on labor management change efforts (Zager & Rosow, 1982), the initial boundaries were drawn around the local union and local factory. Over time, it became apparent that the relevant social boundaries should include organizationally distant activities, such as the corporate headquarters and the international union headquarters. The organizational effectiveness literature (Cameron & Whetten, 1983, Meyer & Gupta, 1994) and the related literature on organizational errors (Perrow, 1984; Vaughan, 1996) focus our attention on critical constituencies, another way to identify critical actors. The research in network analysis (cf. Laumann, Marsden, & Prensky, 1983) provides still another conceptual and methodological way to identify players and their relations in a social system.

Given a list of actors, another step in charting is to distinguish between actors involved in activities and outcomes that are directly versus indirectly involved in the linkage analysis. In the Challenger case, let's assume that the functioning of the solid rocket booster and O-rings was related to the explosion and subsequent disaster. The social system, then, encompasses actors (organizations and people) who have some direct involvement in information or decisions about the O-rings and the solid rocket booster. The principals seem to be the prime contractors—Thiokol and the Marshall Space Center. If we use the criteria of providing information or decisions relevant to the rocket booster or the O-ring, we would include others such as subcontractors to Thiokol and the review procedure within NASA to assess technical integrity.

We also know that Congress and congressional committees are relevant actors. They oversee NASA and affect budgets that filter down to create technical and economic imperatives for subcontractors like Thiokol. These effects, as Vaughan (1996) demonstrated, are important contextual factors in the life of Challenger. However, they are not directly involved in shaping the understandings or decisions about the solid rocket booster or the O-ring. These would be considered to be more indirect. I want to be clear that indirect effects and context are important in understanding Allied Manufacturing, Barings, or ValuJet. My task initially is to define the initial social system for analysis. Focusing on direct effects simplifies getting started.

A third and complementary approach in this chart-making process is to think iteratively. In the ValuJet case, it is not obvious that SabreTech would have been in the initial chart. Over time, there were reasons to introduce this organization. In doing this, it was important to recognize that the boundaries around SabreTech might be redrawn. Remember that a relationship between SabreTech and a potential customer triggered the SabreTech manager to ask shipping personnel to move the canisters. These eventually found their way to Flight 592. This customer, then, should be included in the definition of the social system. In this example, we are looking for actors who may have some direct relation to the sequence of activities and events that led to the crash of Flight 592. The identification process is open and continually iterating.

Time Frame

The next step in this chart making is to think about time. We need to define the social system at different time periods. You probably would interrupt and say that it is clear that time makes sense, but not in the context of chart making. We use a chart to help us sail from Boston to Northeast Harbor or from Macao to Singapore. We want the chart to represent the present, not an outdated chart.

My response to including time in chart making is that a deep knowledge of navigating this route would be facilitated not only by a current chart but also by how the land and markers might have changed over time. This deeper understanding, afforded by looking at charts over time, may provide insights into currents, potential dangers, and new possible routes.

Let's move from metaphors to some more scientific analysis. One of the most striking features of Diane Vaughan's book on the Challenger disaster is the effect of the sequence of shuttle flights prior to the Challenger. Each of these flights was a learning trial. There were problems with the Flight "X"'s O-rings. A solution was identified and implemented. What happened in the next flight?—no problems. There was a different problem with the O-rings in a subsequent flight, and there were some successful "fixes." Although there are many other factors affecting the final outcome, this sequence of flights and the trial-and-error learning is critical to understand the final disaster. It is a way of shaping the meaning of the O-rings for the critical actors. Focusing on the day before the launch as the point of analysis is a mistake. Remember also, in the ValuJet case, there were many "violations" defined by the FAA prior to the Flight 592 incident.

Defining the time period is no easier than defining the relevant actors. The Challenger analysis, as a source of insight into the final outcome, points to looking at recurrent decisions. How far back should you go? In the Challenger case, tracing flights from the initiation of this specific program makes sense. Why? A program is made up of a series

	ValuJet		*SabreTech*
ORGANIZATION	Operations	Activities	Operations
	Marketing	Outcomes	Marketing
	Finance		Finance
GROUP/UNITS	Crew	Activities	ValuJet Operations
	Ground Operations	Outcomes	Shipping
INDIVIDUAL	Pilot	Activities	Workers
	Copilot	Outcomes	Supervisors
	Flight Attendants		Inspectors

Figure 3.4. Chart Making—ValuJet—Internal Organization

of launches in which there is similarity in objectives, technology, and personnel. Earlier NASA programs had different objectives, technology, and personnel. Probably more important, the series of flights preceding the Challenger flight provided an opportunity for most of the relevant actors to develop a shared understanding of the performance of the O-rings and the perceived risk or normal deviancy inherent in these rings. In this case, the learning periods (reviews after launches) throughout the program of launches define the time period.

ValuJet was only 2 years old at the time of the crash. It was going through a rapid growth period. Also, it was receiving a lot of violations from the FAA, and a request had been made within the FAA to review ValuJet's certification. Given that violations represent deviations from organizational practices and may be an indicator of subsequent organizational errors, going back to the beginning of ValuJet or to when violations began to increase rapidly may be one way to mark the time period of ValuJet.

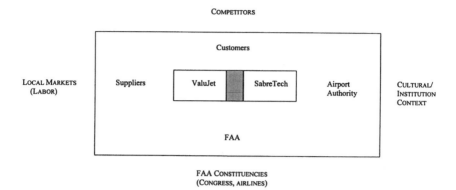

Figure 3.5. Chart Making—ValuJet—External Organization

Another way to identify the time period of the social system is to pay attention to major changes in organizations, people, or technology. In a study I did on tracking organization changes over a 3-year period (Goodman, 1979), there were clear events (e.g., opening up a new production system, major changes in personnel) that were independent of the change effort but that clearly defined very different contexts to understand the change process. These events defined the time periods within the social system for analysis.

I want to reinforce this discussion of how to define the social system using some features of the ValuJet case. Figure 3.4 describes the internal social system at ValuJet and SabreTech. Each is independent, but they were overlapping organizations. Activities and outcomes occur at the individual, group, and organizational level for both organizations. Individual activities by SabreTech supervisors and workers affect the overall operations of the project team that is reconditioning the ValuJet planes and, in turn, they affect the organizational activities and outcomes for SabreTech. Similarly, some of these individual activities and outcomes will directly affect the outcomes of ValuJet.

Figure 3.5 illustrates potential players in the external social system that are relevant for the analysis of the crash of Flight 592. We know from the previous account that the customers of SabreTech and the FAA engage in activities that may affect the activities and outcomes of different levels described in Figure 3.4. The groups listed outside the rectangle, such as competitors or constituencies, are part of the contextual analysis. Their effects on activities and outcomes are indirect and

Beginning of ValuJet	Report by FAA on Violations	SabreTech Contract	Crash Flight 592
(October 23, 1993)	(February 1996)	(Not Available)	(May 11, 1996)

Figure 3.6. Chart Making—ValuJet—Time

important. For example, government funding of the FAA partially accounts for the number of inspectors, which may affect the activities and outcomes of ValuJet or SabreTech.

Figure 3.6 provides the time line for the ValuJet analysis. It reflects a basic argument in this chapter that understanding linkages requires looking at different systems over time.

Concluding Thoughts

- The concepts of outcome coupling and feedback systems can help us in our exploration of linkages across units and/or levels.

- Each concept has a set of analytic questions that should help us understand how changes in activities and outcomes at one level affect other levels.

- In examining outcomes, we want to focus on whether the metrics are the same, forms of organizing, the number of intermediary outcomes, the extent to which activities are programmed, and time lags.

- In examining negative feedback loops, we want to focus on whether desired behaviors are stated, whether monitoring systems exist, and whether organizational actors respond to gaps between desired and actual states and the delay in responding.

- In examining positive feedback, we want to focus on initial conditions, the form of the accelerating cycles, and the timing of these cycles.

- Outcome coupling is the first step in a linkage analysis. It identifies structural properties of the linkage that may facilitate or inhibit changes in activities and outcomes at one unit or level in affecting activities and outcomes at other units or levels.

- The feedback systems are one set of tools for understanding some of the mechanisms that underlie the basic linkage question.

- The process of defining the social system in terms of critical actors, internal and external to the organization and over time, sets the stage for the linkage analysis.

- This process of definition can be informed by organizational theory, empirical research, and experience. However, it remains a complex and challenging task. There are likely to be many iterations in defining the social system.

Conversation Three

You: I think the concepts such as outcome coupling or positive feedback systems are interesting concepts, but I don't see how they fit together. Draw me the diagram.

PSG: I do not think there is some neatly ordered way to represent the connections among these tools or concepts. There is a strong institutional orientation in our field to build that kind of structure with boxes and arrows, but I don't see it in analyzing linkages. Think of them as tools in your analysis box. Different linkage problems and different organizational contexts will require different combinations of tools.

You: But there must be some way of ordering these concepts.

PSG: There is, in a temporal sense. I said that you need to begin by building an initial chart by defining the social system. I think that is the way to begin. However, I did say explicitly and implicitly that this initial chart will surely change.

It seems to me that the next step is to think about the elements in outcome coupling—metrics, forms of organizing, number of intermediary activities, level of programmed activities, and time. These factors should help us to understand more about why Barings went bankrupt.

You: What about the role of the feedback systems?

PSG: I think they are very important, and they will play a role in our analysis of organizational errors, change, and learning. You might think of defining the social system and applying the dimensions of outcome coupling (Figure 3.2) as a way of building the basic elements of the chart. On one hand, the social system definitions are general. On the other hand, mapping the elements of the outcome coupling provides a fairly detailed account of relevant structures. The feedback processes provide the dynamic elements to the chart. In some ways, the feedback systems serve as the wind and currents, dynamic phenomena that have both order and disorder.

You: These tools and the way you talk about them seem very *ex post*. How can you use them to intellectually organize and then explain some organizational phenomena?

PSG: I think the tools can be used in an *ex ante* or *ex post* fashion. In this book, I am telling stories and then doing linkage analysis. Therefore, I am presenting everything in an *ex post* manner. But the two tools I have delineated can be used in planning research and generating propositions. For example, if I have two conditions in which the outcome metrics are the same (different), the form of organizing is additive (reciprocal), and there are few (many) intermediary activities, it is pretty clear where impacts across units or levels will be observable.

You: What about the other tools you mentioned in Table 3.1?

PSG: The dilemma we have in writing or in learning is the serial process we must follow. In Table 3.1, I wanted to indicate what is in the tool box, but I could only develop carefully a few tools at a time. Also, I want us to practice with these tools (outcome coupling and feedback systems) in Chapter 4 before I introduce some new tools. Think about this as a cumulative process. New tools will be presented in Chapter 5 and 6, and, each time, we will integrate these with the ones previously presented, in the context of a specific linkage problem. My goal is to keep the number of tools small. Different problem areas—organizational errors, organizational change, and organizational learning—may require different combinations of tools.

4 Organizational Errors

This chapter is about organizational errors. I want to apply some of the tools we are developing for linkage analyses to the domain of errors. The goals are to better understand how linkage analysis works and to develop some new perspectives in thinking about errors in organizations. Two cases are analyzed—Barings and ValuJet.

Organizational errors are an excellent setting for understanding linkages. Often, they deal with individual activities (e.g., trading at Barings, removing the oxygen canisters at ValuJet) that have significant negative consequences for the organization. Our interest is in understanding the conditions when these individual activities will or will not have consequences for other units in the organization.

Let's start this exploration by delineating the meaning of organizational errors. When you think about organizational errors, names like Three Mile Island, Chernobyl, and Bhopal come to mind. Our introductory descriptions of ValuJet and, of course, the Challenger disaster are other examples of errors with which you may have been familiar.

Actually, organizational errors are much more pervasive. We pay attention to Chernobyl, Bhopal, or Challenger because they are physical disasters. People died. A cursory reading of the newspaper would illustrate many other examples of organizational errors. Barings, a venerable British Bank, 233 years in operation, goes bankrupt. But what about Daiwa and Sumitomo? These organizations also experienced

AUTHOR'S NOTE: This chapter was written with and reflects current research with Rangaraj Ramanujam.

huge financial losses in similar ways due to errors in routine internal operations. If you go on the Internet to www.nhtsa.dot.gov, you will be amazed by the number of auto recalls. Hudson Beef, which had to close down an entire plant because of infected beef products, is another example.

There has been significant work on organizational errors. Perrow (1984) talked about accidents as a "failure in the subsystem, or the system as a whole, that damages more than one unit and in doing so disrupts the ongoing or future output of the system" (p. 66). His concept of normal accidents has been very influential. He argued that there are unexpected interactions of multiple failures in a system that cannot be anticipated and that lead to negative consequences. Other researchers have framed this research error in terms of error-free operations (LaPorte & Consolini, 1991; Roberts, 1990). Proponents of "high reliability" have focused on structural and process features that lead to high-reliability systems. Weick, Sutcliffe, and Obstfeld's (1999) portrayal of "mindfulness" provides a newer theoretical perspective on error-free operations. Vaughan's (1996) research on the Challenger launch is outstanding both because of its detailed tracking of a significant error and in the weaving together of a broad set of institutional, cultural, structural, and process events that affected the decision to launch the Challenger in January 1986.

My analysis draws heavily on this literature. At the same time, however, it diverges in the following ways: First, although negative outcomes can be both physical and nonphysical, most of the literature has focused on negative physical consequences. There can be financial and reputational tragedies as well as human tragedies. We focus on physical and nonphysical errors. Second, much of the literature has focused on complex technical systems such as nuclear power plants and nuclear aircraft carriers. Thus, the theoretical perspectives were influenced by the central role of technology in these organizations. Although these types of organizations are important to study, there is obviously a wide range of organizations in which the technology is not the principal driver. Contrast Three Mile Island and the Challenger. In the former, you have a dominant, complex technological system with tightly coupled subcomponents. In the Challenger, you have this complicated web of organizations responsible for building, launching, and bringing back a sophisticated, technological vehicle. These different settings should provide different insights about organizational errors. My focus is on organizations in which the technology system is not dominant. Finally, much of the literature has concentrated on actual errors, that is, situations that have led to negative consequences. We delineate different types of actual and latent errors. The interaction among different types of errors is an important part of a linkage analysis of organizational errors.

Defining Organizational Errors

Organizational errors refer to the failure of the organization to correct deviations from expectations, which, in turn, results in actual or potential negative consequences for the organization. A critical element I discuss in the Barings case was the organization's failure to manage deviations. The deviations of the trader were known. Why were they not corrected?

Expectations refer to shared understandings about work activities. In the Barings case, there were clear expectations about trading limits and the balances that should appear in accounts at the end of the day. In the ValuJet case, there was a statement in the work order about the use of safety caps on the oxygen canisters. Expectations have their source in formal organizational procedures. Regulatory bodies such as the Food and Drug Administration, the National Safety Board, and the Security and Exchange Commission also are sources of expectations. Expectations, of course, are dynamic; their meanings are changed by different interest groups and by time. Also, expectations may or may not be correct. A trading limit may be faulty, exposing a bank to large financial losses.

Deviations refer to work activities that differ from expectations. A trader exceeding assigned limits is a deviation. In another example, a bank manages custodial accounts for a customer, who has indicated the dates on which certain securities must be traded. The bank fails to effect the trade, the market drops, and the customer, and subsequently the bank, suffer financial losses. Other forms of deviations, such as intent to sabotage or defraud an organization, are not part of this discussion of errors.

Monitoring is an important component in organizational errors. The definition of organizational errors deals with the failure of the organization to take corrective action. Corrective action can only occur if deviations can be detected. Errors and negative consequences can occur with and without monitoring. In the Barings case, there were both clear trading limits (expectations) and monitoring systems to pick up account balances on a daily basis.

Remember that errors and negative consequences can occur without monitoring. Here are two instances. In an automobile factory or beef processing facility, formal measurement/sampling systems detect poor quality, but the systems do not conduct 100% inspection. Occasionally, a defective product gets through, and there are subsequent penalties for the company. In the ValuJet case, there was no system monitoring shipping clerks' behavior with respect to hazardous material.

Corrective action refers to organizational actions taken to reduce errors. One interesting question in the Barings case was, "Given there were expectations (trading limits) and monitoring system data about exceeding the limits (monitoring), why did corrective behavior not follow?" That is one of the most exciting and interesting questions about errors. In the literature, researchers have pointed to organizational culture (Vaughan, 1996), lack of training (Shrivastava, 1987), organizational politics (Sagan, 1993), and redundancy (Ramanujam & Goodman, 1998) as reasons for organizational inaction. This point is explored further in this chapter.

Negative consequences are the last component of the definition. In introducing organizational errors, we pointed to the broader view of negative consequences, which includes indicators such as loss of reputation, financial losses, and survival of the organization, as well as physical losses.

Typology of Organizational Errors

This definition of organizational errors leads to an interesting typology of errors (see Figure 4.1). The typology (Ramanujam & Goodman, 1998) is important because it identifies different types of errors. Let's start at the bottom of Figure 4.1 and work up. Organizational errors represent deviations from expectations that are monitored and to which no corrective action is taken, resulting in significant negative outcomes. The Barings case includes all of these features. A latent organizational error also has all of the previous features, but no negative consequences. For example, a trader is outside of the limits, but the market moves in a direction that prevents any losses, for the time being.

A different type of error is in the design of the transaction measurement system. For example, assume that the bank's monitoring system reports on transactions weekly versus daily. Trading outside the limits for a few days would not be picked up by the measurement system, but it may lead to significant negative consequences. Latent errors in the next category represent undetected deviations that do not lead immediately to negative organizational consequences.

Also, there can be errors in process design. A bank has a process in place to determine a customer's creditworthiness, which is faulty, but this is not known. The expectations about the process are clear, employees follow the process, and no deviations exist. However, defects in the process interact with the size of the loan or the type of customer, and large losses occur. This is an error in process design.

Problem solving errors are quite common in organizational life. In these cases, the goals are understood but the means to reach them are not well understood or agreed on. There are no expectations. The choices are uncertain and risky, as in the case of new product introductions or new technology. The decision maker uses the appropriate information and processes, selects an option, and experiences negative consequences.

Why enumerate this typology of errors? In the first place, the literature tends not to differentiate among these forms of errors. Second, the classification suggests there may be different antecedents of errors and the linkage analysis may be different. For example, in the case of "organizational errors," deviations occur and are noted, but no corrective action follows. In process or measurement errors, there are no deviations, but negative consequences occur. Third, different types of errors may interact with each other in a particular setting and generate new errors. This is an important implication for analyses in this chapter.

Analyzing Barings and ValuJet

Barings

At the time of its collapse in 1995, Barings was a 233-year-old investment bank based in London. In 1992, it began trading in securities in

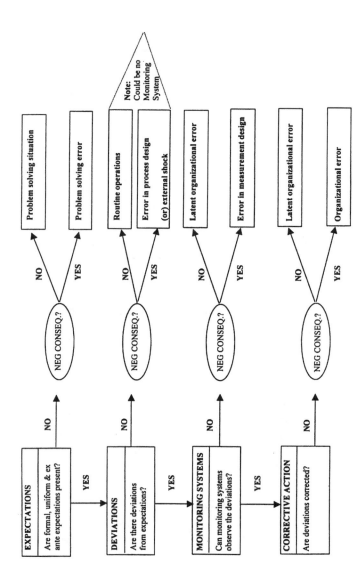

Figure 4.1. A Framework for Organizational Errors

Singapore. The trader in this unit—Nick Leeson—was allowed to carry on trading on behalf of the bank as long as his trading activities satisfied two conditions. First, he had to square his positions at the end of each day. This meant that at the end of the day, if he had an oversold (overbought) position, he had to buy (sell) securities so that the net position was square. This rule was meant to ensure that the bank did not expose itself to risks due to overnight changes in the market prices of securities. Second, at no point during the day could the total value of the trades exceed a prespecified limit. This intraday trading limit was in place to maintain the risk exposure at acceptable levels.

Over time, Leeson began to exceed these limits. The intraday trading volumes consistently exceeded the prespecified limits. Furthermore, Leeson did not square his positions at the end of each day. The bank was thus exposed to significant risks due to potential market volatility. During this period, the corporate headquarters received periodic reports about the trading operations in Singapore. At the very least, these reports contained information that should have alerted them to the possibility of deviations in the Singapore operations. In addition, a review of the unit's operations by the internal control unit expressed serious concerns about the observed trading practices and the fact that the trading and settlement activities were controlled by the key trader. However, the senior management made no effort to bring Leeson's trading to within prespecified limits. In fact, they continued to transfer margin money to support the trading and did not separate the trading and settlement activities (Ministry of Finance Report, 1995). By the end of January 1995, Leeson had accumulated more than 28,000 contracts amounting to $29 billion. Most of these contracts represented bets that the Nikkei index would not fall below 18,000 points. Unforeseen events led to a steep fall in Japanese stock prices and brought the index to below 18,000 points. Barings lost $1.4 billion and was forced into bankruptcy.

Let me add some other contextual information to help you follow the analysis. This builds on our discussion of "defining the social system" in Chapter 3.

1. The trigger. In the beginning of 1995, Leeson had accumulated contracts equaling $7 billion of Japanese stocks and $22 billion of Japanese interest futures. When an earthquake occurred at Kobe, Japan, prices and interest rates declined in response to the negative impact of this natural disaster on the Japanese economy. Within a month, the bank was exposed to losses of $1.4 billion and was forced into bankruptcy. The trigger, an earthquake and the market's reaction, interacted with large exposed positions, resulting in substantial losses. If the earthquake had not occurred and the stock market had not reacted adversely to this event, Barings may or may not have suffered losses. Trading in an environment with random exogenous shocks is different from a market with predictable fluctuations over time.

2. *Defining the social system—internal.* The original Barings Bank (BP) had been in business for more than 200 years. It recruited "gentlemen" bankers from the best universities. Their work was in building long-term relationships with large organizations to provide a variety of financial services (raising capital). Barings Securities (BS), the new unit, recruited traders from different educational and social environments who wanted to play in the high-risk game of trading. These were different organizations in terms of people, tasks, clients, and history. Organizationally, BS was a separate, independent entity within the Barings structure. Using our earlier terminology, it is an additive unit. Within BS was the Singapore office (BFS), which was an additive unit within BS.

A division between BP and BS grew as BS began to make huge profits. Between 1987 and 1989, BS accounted for almost 80% of BP's overall profits. This resource contribution shifted power within the organization and provided greater autonomy to BS (Pfeffer & Salancik, 1978). Conflict between BS and BP was reflected in the resignation of the BS CEO and attempts to restrict BS. The environment Leeson operated in was one of conflicts over power, autonomy, and control. The high performance of BS was an important lever in its ability to remain independent.

3. *Defining the social system—external.* This case unfolds in a global market context. In addition to customers, there were major financial exchanges in Singapore, Tokyo, and Osaka where trading took place. Also, regulatory groups from the Bank of England, Bank of International Settlements, the European Union, Singapore, and Japan were involved. All these groups are part of the social system for understanding the unfolding of events. For example, the Bank of International Settlements in Basel, Switzerland, wrote to BP seeking explanations for hold-

ing such large positions exposed in the market. Such a letter is a signal of potential problems. The Bank of England imposes limits on British banks in terms of the percentage of their capital that could be allocated to trading activity. This regulatory bank gave informal concessions to BP about this limit. The concessions created some ambiguity about whether BP was exceeding prespecified limits.

4. Defining the time period. In this case, defining the time period seems quite straightforward. We could begin when BFS began trading in 1992 or when Leeson came to work for BFS in 1992. Both were the beginning of a series of activities, events, and outcomes that led to the final disaster.

5. Types of errors. Before we ask the "why did this happen" question, it is probably useful to examine the types of errors in the Barings case (Figure 4.1). To remind the reader, organizational errors occur when there are expectations, deviations, monitoring, no corrective action, and negative consequences. There were clear expectations about trading behavior. Leeson could maintain unhedged positions within certain limits during the day and could not maintain unhedged positions overnight. Evidence indicates the trader was deviating from these rules. On the other hand, Leeson had a trading account 88888, which included large unhedged positions that exposed Barings to large potential losses. The bank's reporting system, partly through Leeson's initiatives, did not capture the level of risk exposure to the bank. This would be labeled, in our terminology, a measurement error.

In addition, there were faulty process mechanisms that were permitted to remain in operation by the highest levels of the bank. One of the most obvious was that Leeson had control of both the trading and settlement operations. This example would correspond to a process design error. Latent errors occurred when Leeson deviated from expectations but made a profit or avoided a loss. Problem-solving errors occurred when the trader made unsuccessful trades.

The Barings case represents a combination of different errors. Also, the interrelations among the errors are important for understanding the eventual bankruptcy of the bank, that is, measurement and design errors may contribute to organizational errors, and vice versa.

Why did this happen? How could a 200-year-old, highly respected British investment bank go bankrupt? In organizational linkage terminology, we want to know how activities at the trader level, BFS level, and BS level affected the total organization? How were activities, events, and outcomes at one level able to bring down a 200-year-old institution?

A key idea is not to focus primarily on Leeson's behavior. That is only one piece of the puzzle. The most senior management knew there were problems with the BFS organization, but there were no attempts to change the situation. Large payments were made between BS and BFS without clear understanding or ability by management to reconcile some of these transactions. External auditors and regulators pointed out potential problems that were acknowledged but ignored. The picture, then, is a set of complicated relationships within Barings and between Barings and their external constituencies. The time period for these activities, events, and outcomes begins with the deregulation of the financial markets in 1986 and the organizing of BS. The real story begins with Leeson's move to BFS in 1992.

Using our tools, we can unbundle some of these complicated relationships.

1. Outcome coupling. A discussion of the relation between outcomes at different levels of analysis was introduced in Chapter 3. The premise is that outcomes at different levels can be characterized in terms of metrics, forms of organizing, intermediary activities, and so on. In the Barings case, the metrics are the same between BFS and BP. There are no intermediary activities between profits and losses at BFS and BP other than the accounting system that accumulates information from operating units. Also, there is little, if any, time lag between a reported profit in BFS and the record of that profit at BP. In this situation, there is a direct and immediate impact on changes in one level on another.

2. Positive feedback loops. Here, the basic idea is that an increase in one variable (A) causes increases in another variable (B), which causes an increase in the first variable (A). Positive feedback loops have no equilibrium. They push a system in an accelerated direction to an unstable condition.

Initial conditions can be a powerful determinant of activities, events, and outcomes over an extended period of time. Indeed, the effect over time may not be proportional to the initial condition. The initial condition in this analysis was Leeson's success in trading for the bank's customers. Leeson's success caused BP to request him to trade on behalf of the bank. This move reinforced Leeson's positive position and legitimated Leeson's role in taking risks on behalf of the bank. Leeson's initial "halo" persisted through much of the case and is an important element in understanding the potential contradictions in this case.

The accelerating cycles in the positive feedback loops are evident throughout. In the first 7 months of 1994, BFS reported profits of $30 million compared to $1.6 million for all of 1992. Leeson was seen as the major contributor to the huge increase in profitability. These dramatic, positive changes reinforced Leeson's personal goals, motivation, and self-esteem and accelerated his trading behavior. The increases in profitability attributed to Leeson increased his legitimation by senior bank personnel, which, in turn, accelerated his trading, which increased his star quality and relative independence. Other events such as BS and BFS blocking attempts by BP to gain more control of their operations and their ability to block the internal report that recommended separating Leeson's trading and settlement activities all served to reinforce the independence of Leeson's trading activities and of the securities operations. In Chapter 3, I indicated that there may be time lags before the acceleration cycles begin. In this case, they seemed to have initiated right after Leeson's initial successes and his move to trade on behalf of the bank.

3. Negative feedback loops. These loops move a system toward an equilibrium. Desired states are compared to actual states, and any discrepancy leads to system change and movement toward an equilibrium.

In the Barings case, the negative feedback loops did not function as one might predict. Let's look at this first from Leeson's perspective. There is evidence that he engaged in large, unhedged transactions that were in violation of expectations about acceptable trading behavior. However, he was a star performer and, by all accounts, one of the most powerful individuals in BFS. Also, there was conflict between BFS and BP and a movement by BFS toward greater autonomy. Given this setting, determining whether positions were appropriately hedged or whether Leeson was trading in the appropriate instruments seems really to have been based on Leeson's construction of the situation rather than norms or rules promulgated by BP.

In the cases of losses, it is harder to reconstruct why the feedback process did not work. Large losses generate clear, negative feedback signals. One strategy might be to try to reduce high-risk trading activities and to try to balance accounts. However, Leeson accelerated his high-risk trading. Why? Escalation theory (Staw, 1981) provides a useful explanation. Leeson is highly visible as a star and highly committed to his role as a trader. Negative feedback in this condition stimulates accelerated high-risk trading behavior. This is an interesting intersection where denying negative feedback accelerates positive feedback cycles.

We also need to understand Leeson in the context of other players in the social system. The attempt to remove him from performing both trading and settlement activities failed. BP advanced Leeson large amounts of money in 1994-1995 without much required documentation. This was a clear signal for continuing his current behavior. Also, he was able to make transactions in account 88888.

My basic argument is that Leeson discounted information in the negative feedback loops. He was a star. His unit (BFS) had successfully resisted control efforts from BP. The bank's action (i.e., the advances) legitimated his behavior.

A more interesting question is why management at all levels behaved the way they did. Using the negative feedback loop process, we look at three events that displayed deviations, but these deviations did not initiate action that would close the gap between desired and actual outcomes.

First, there was an internal audit report by BP that recommended changing the practice of Leeson effecting both trades and settlements. The report and recommendation had been widely circulated at all levels and in the relevant locations (e.g., Singapore and London). A year later, nothing had been implemented. Why? One explanation concerns the phenomenon of diffusion of responsibility (Latane & Darley, 1970). If there are large numbers of people who know about a problem, one implication is that people feel that others will take care of the situation, and, thus, nothing happens. This explanation appears in the Bank of England analysis (Bank of England, 1995) of the Barings case. Another explanation focuses on power. Leeson was in a powerful position in BFS, and BFS was in a power confrontation with BP. One way for BFS to state and enhance its power position was to disregard the proposal. Successfully warding off any attempts to control its operation only served to enhance BFS's feeling of invulnerability and to accelerate high-risk activities.

Another example concerns funding of BFS by BP. From 1993 to 1995, Leeson made funding requests to support his trading activities. For example, during the first 2 months of 1995, Leeson had accumulated contracts equaling $7 billion of Japanese stocks and $22 billion of Japanese interest futures. For these contracts, Leeson had to place large margin deposits that were supplied by BP London. A startling finding in the Bank of England report (Bank of England, 1995) was that requests for these funds by BFS were not well documented, it was unclear to managers in treasury or settlements whether the sums were for client or house trading, and there was no credit review process of this funding, yet it was approved. Again, this event is similar to the prior example in that this situation was known to a variety of managers in different units.

Why did this situation occur? In negative feedback terms, there is a discrepancy between a desired state of processes that require adequate documentation and review before releasing funds to BFS and actually what happened. The question of why this happened is the same. Why were the discrepancies between desired and actual practice ignored? One explanation may be tied to Leeson's star quality. He was seen as the source of a large portion of the profitability of Barings, and one might treat stars differently from other employees, that is, one is less likely to challenge his requests or the documentation of his requests. Another reason may be diffusion of responsibility that was mentioned previously. Someone else has responsibility for monitoring these funds transfers. A different explanation concerns the escalation process. This assumes that prior commitments to provide funds from BP to BFS may lead to accelerated commitments, particularly in the light of negative information that Leeson had exposed the bank to large risk positions.

Although we will never know the precise reason for the behavior of the bank's managers, the perspective from Leeson's side is quite compelling. He made continual requests for large amounts of funds that he received over a period of 2 years. What is the signal he received? Continue on your present course.

Summary. The Barings case is an example of a system out of control. There were accelerating forces driving the bank into greater positions of risk exposure. The rates of change were not small incremental effects

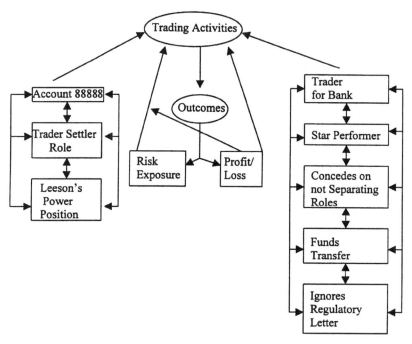

Figure 4.2. Barings in Motion

but accelerating nonlinear changes. The drivers were a series of actors, activities, and events interacting and reinforcing each other over time.

Another way to think about Barings is that there was a body of growing and interacting errors: *design errors,* such as the inadequate process for credit review of fund exchanges between BP and BFS or Leeson's joint roles of trading and settling; *measurement errors,* such as the inability to track account 88888; and *latent errors,* such as maintaining unhedged positions. Each error by itself was not fatal. However, they interact and reinforce each other. The ability to do trading and settlement helped Leeson create the 88888 account, which, in turn, permitted unhedged positions, which, in turn, created other forms of latent errors as the cycle continued and accelerated. The earthquake and the market decline triggered the financial disaster. If it had not been for this unexpected event, we cannot be sure when and whether the financial disaster would have occurred. However, we do know the bank's risk exposure was growing at an accelerated rate.

Figure 4.2 tries to capture some of the complexity and chaos in the Barings system. The central portion of the figure focuses on the trading—initially an individual (Leeson) level set of activities, events, and outcomes. Trading initially was successful, which accelerated trading activities both in amounts and types of trading. Losses, which appeared later, also can accelerate trading through the escalation process.

The left side of the figure shows a set of structural features such as account 88888, the combined trader settler role, and Leeson's power position that serve as a self-reinforcing system and a force for accelerating his trading behavior.

The right side of the figure shows a set of structural features and activities that are self-reinforcing from BP's perspective. For example, the perception of Leeson as a star performer facilitates the process of funds transfer between BP and BFS, which, in turn, facilitates the perception of him as a star performer. The acceleration of this funds transfer is consistent with ignoring regulatory inquiries about the bank's ability to deal with high exposure levels. This subsystem of activities individually and together reinforces trading behavior designed to accelerate the bank's risk exposure.

ValuJet

I want to introduce a different case on errors and linkages by briefly revisiting the ValuJet story. It is such a contrast to Barings that a short visit will be valuable.

On May 11, 1996, a Douglas DC-9-32 crashed in the Everglades about 10 minutes after takeoff from Miami International Airport. All 110 people on the plane were killed. An analysis was conducted by the National Transportation Safety Board (NTSB):

> The probable causes of the accident, resulting in a fire in the Class D cargo compartment from the actuation of one or more oxygen generators improperly carried as cargo, were: (1) the failure of SabreTech to properly prepare, package, identify, and track unexpended chemical oxygen generators before presenting them to ValuJet for carriage; (2) the failure of ValuJet to properly oversee its contract maintenance program to ensure compliance with maintenance, maintenance training, and hazardous materials requirements and practices; and (3) the failure of Federal Aviation Administration

(FAA) to require smoke detection and fire suppression in Class D cargo compartments. (NTSB, 1997)

In Figure 2.2 in Chapter 2, the ValuJet story was portrayed in six classes of events. The mechanics from SabreTech were reconditioning three MD-80s for ValuJet. The first cycle of activities was to remove and replace oxygen canisters from the plane and complete the necessary paperwork. One activity in removing canisters is to insert a safety cap. Another activity could have been to label the canisters as hazardous. A final activity in this cycle was signing off the work order by the mechanics, supervisors, and inspectors. There is ambiguity in the accounts of ValuJet (NTSB, 1997) about whether inspectors were required to sign off. The idea is if people had to sign off, they might have observed that the safety caps were not on. The next cycle of activities concerned moving the canisters to SabreTech shipping. The third cycle concerned boxing and labeling the canisters in shipping. The fourth event was the physical movement of the canisters to Flight 592. The last two events deal with the acceptance and placement of the canisters on the plane.

Let me add some other contextual information to help you follow this analysis.

1. The trigger. The specific trigger was either the placement of the canisters in the forward hold or the movement of the canisters during take-off, which ignited one or more of the canisters. Because there was no early warning system or suppression system in that part of the plane, it would have been very difficult for the crew to realize the problem in time for an emergency landing. The trigger in this case and in Barings was not intentional.

2. Defining the social system—internal (see Figure 3.4, Chapter 3). A key feature in this case was the outsourcing arrangement between ValuJet and SabreTech. I include the SabreTech relationship as "internal" because maintenance is a core function of an airline. If one chooses to outsource this function, it is clearly critical to the internal functioning of the airline. ValuJet assigned jobs to SabreTech (e.g., reconfiguring airplanes), the planes were returned to ValuJet, and future maintenance problems led to new job assignments for SabreTech. The control of this relationship was the responsibility of ValuJet.

One cause of this disaster from the perspective of the NTSB was the failure of ValuJet to manage, control, and monitor the activities of SabreTech (note the parallels between BP and BFS). One reason for this lack of control and monitoring may be what was happening at ValuJet. ValuJet was going through rapid change. In 2½ years, the company moved from 2 to 51 planes. That is an enormous change. Maintaining some order in this system would be a major challenge. This is not a highly rationalized organization looking at refinement in excellence. This is an organization experiencing rapid change, elements of chaos, and struggling to maintain some semblance of perceived order (see Figure 3.4 in Chapter 3 for other elements in the internal system).

3. Defining the social system—external. These relationships primarily focus on regulators, namely the FAA, and the interagency relationship between the FAA and NTSB. First, early in 1996, there was growing concern within the FAA about maintenance and operations at ValuJet. One recommendation was to recertify the airline, which means they would have to stop operations, but it was never implemented. Instead, a 3-month special inspection was initiated in February. In other words, there was awareness of potentially serious problems. Second, the NTSB report was critical of the FAA for having designed inadequate staffing levels for monitoring airlines in the southern region, for not sufficiently overseeing ValuJet's operation, and for not implementing prior NTSB recommendations concerning the use of fire sensors and fire suppression devices in aircraft. These interagency relationships were part of the external context for this analysis.

4. Defining the time period. In terms of time, we would track this social system from the creation of ValuJet and from the beginning of the SabreTech relationship. Both the rapid growth of ValuJet and the history of violations indicate that the initiation of the airline in 1993 would be the appropriate time to begin the analysis of Flight 592 (see Figure 3.6 in Chapter 3).

5. Types of errors. What was going on at SabreTech and ValuJet? Were there expectations about the appropriate behaviors? I think the answer is yes (NTSB, 1997). In the ValuJet work order, there is a statement about installing safety caps on the firing pin. In the MD-80 manual, there are statements about how to store canisters and how to deal with expended canisters that have certain hazardous chemical properties. There were expectations for shipping personnel on how to deal with hazardous material. And the ramp supervisor and the copilot were trained to identify hazardous material, even if it is not so labeled.

Now, you might say, well, no one reads manuals, or companies do a lot of training but that training does not get played out in day-to-day operations. Although that observation is true, these canisters were considered potentially hazardous material. Also, my intent is to establish whether the expectations (e.g., training to identify hazardous material) were presented, not whether people acted on them. We can assume that these were expectations for SabreTech and ValuJet personnel across the activities I have described.

Deviations occurred at each event. The mechanics did not put on the safety caps, they signed off on the work that was not done correctly, and they stored the canisters incorrectly. The shipping personnel could have labeled the materials as hazardous, which would have precluded sending them by plane to Atlanta. Finally, the ramp agent and copilot could have prevented this material from being loaded on this plane.

There was no direct monitoring system for any of these activities. There was no monitoring system for measuring whether mechanics put on caps or whether ramp supervisors put hazardous material on airplanes. The only measuring systems present were indirectly imposed through industry-wide government regulations. Government safety inspectors review practices and submit reports that may lead to violations and penalties. There were special investigations of ValuJet initiated by the FAA in 1996 because of concerns about the company's safety practices. These individual measures may capture management's attention and lead to corrective action. But here we are focusing on a specific series of events. There is no real-time information system capturing the unfolding deviations depicted previously.

In this case, there was no corrective action, which is not surprising, given that there was no monitoring information concerning the deviance. The absence of any monitoring information reinforces current behavior. Other reasons why there does not seem to be high-level vigilance on these activities are (a) these are not the major day-to-day activities of ValuJet and (b) the activities were subcontracted to another organization. The major day-to-day activities were getting customers on planes, getting planes in and out at reasonable times, and doing this economically and safely.

What kinds of errors do we see in the ValuJet case? There are design, measurement, and organizational errors. Many are latent errors. The canisters without any safety caps lying around in the work area and shipping department represent one example. And although outsourcing is a common business practice, it requires some reasonable control system. This means that ValuJet needed to put in a system to ensure that SabreTech mechanics and supervisors followed procedures about hazardous materials and that ValuJet had monitoring systems to assess compliance with these procedures. Because adequate control systems and measurement systems were both absent, we have examples of design and measurement errors.

Let's go back to some of the tools for organizational linkages that we used on the Barings case and see how they fit here.

1. Outcome coupling. There are five features of outcome coupling—the similarity of metrics, the form of organizing, the number of intermediary connections, the programmed nature of activities, and time. In this case, the metrics of outcomes across activities are very different. The outcome for the SabreTech personnel is the removal of the canisters and the overall reconfiguration of the plane. The outcome for shipping was the movement of the boxes to the plane. The outcomes on Flight 592 were a disaster. In all these cases, the outcomes are in different metrics. In the Barings case, the outcomes were always the same—profits or losses.

The next issue concerns the form of organizing. In ValuJet, the outcomes are arranged in a loosely coupled, horizontal, sequential flow. There are cycles of intermediary activities—the removal of the canisters, the movement to shipping, the storage and labeling at shipping, the movement and loading of the canisters, and the takeoff of Flight 592. There is no programmed order in the sequence. If the mechanics had been following the manual, the hazardous materials may have been disposed of in a special way and not sent to shipping. If shipping had defined the canisters as hazardous, they would not have been routed to one of the ValuJet planes. The timing also was very loose. There was no schedule. There were delays in moving the canisters from the work area to shipping. The intervention by the manager to clean up the shipping area moved the canisters, but this was an exogenous event generated by a visit by another customer. The manager wanted the area to be clean. The visit by the customer had no temporal connection to ValuJet.

2. Positive feedback. This can accelerate systems activities. Typically, there are initial conditions that seem to shape the course of events over time. In the Barings case, Leeson's initial success as a trader created the context for most of the subsequent operations. Here, we are looking at fairly routine production operations of which replacing the canisters is one of many activities. There does not seem to be any incident, be it major or minor, that drives the rest of the story. Also, there are the same types of errors (e.g., design, measurement) that we saw in the Barings case. Although these errors clearly create the conditions for the crash of Flight 592, there are not the same direct interactions among these errors that drove the positive feedback cycle we observed in the Barings case.

3. Negative feedback. This moves a system back to equilibrium. It identifies discrepancies and creates both the motivation and direction for corrective action. Here, there are no monitoring systems to flag deviations. Indeed, the problem is that potential information that might indicate deviations is declining over time. The word "repairable" was placed on the box with canisters by the mechanics. When the shipping clerk received the canisters, there was no explanation about the hazardous nature of the contents. The word "empty" was introduced by the shipping personnel to describe the canisters. When the ramp agent received the material, the label indicated that "aircraft parts" were being shipped back to ValuJet's Atlanta base. Two things seem to be going on. On one hand, there is limited and incorrect information available as we move to the final point where the copilot lets the canisters on board Flight 592. On the other hand, there is no introduction of new information that would have warned any of the parties about the nature of the cargo.

Given this context, the picture we have is a set of loosely connected events. The connection between events and outcomes is also loose. The canisters were not destined for Flight 592. Even if they had been placed on Flight 592, they might not have ignited. As discussed previously, any number of interventions might have changed the course of events. In the Barings case, there really is energy. The energy is directed to making bigger and hopefully more profitable trades. In ValuJet, there is no sense of energy. There are events that come together. But the linkages are loose and the linkages are difficult to predict.

Concluding Thoughts

- Organizational errors are a pervasive part of organizational life. Although the literature has focused on complex technical systems, errors are pervasive in all organizations. Our focus on Barings and ValuJet portrays errors in a setting in which social and organizational systems dominate. Errors occur from humans operating in different organizational arrangements, not from the failure of complex technical systems.

- The typology of errors provides a good mapping of the different types of errors that can occur in organizations. Most of the attention in the literature has been on physical errors that have significant negative consequences. It is important to determine whether these negative consequences are design, measurement, or organizational errors. Also, latent errors are another prevalent form of error. In our two cases, there were multiple forms of errors. In the Barings case, interactions among these different forms of errors contributed to the final failure or bankruptcy of this institution. In ValuJet, the interaction among errors was present but was a less dominant force in the final outcome.

- The initial strategy of identifying the (a) key activities, events, and outcomes, and (b) appropriate social system helped set up the analysis for Barings and ValuJet.

- The next set of conceptual tools—outcome coupling, positive feedback loops, and negative feedback loops—provided a powerful way to explain and possibly predict the negative consequences in the Barings case. Analyzing why the negative feedback systems did not work at Barings or diagramming the factors driving the positive feedback cycles represent ways linkage analysis provides new insights into the occurrence of errors.

  The ValuJet case was presented as a contrast. Although our tools provide some insights on what happened, the activities, events, and outcomes are loosely coupled and difficult to predict *ex ante*.

Conversation Four

You: The two examples seem dramatically different. Do you think your use of tools such as outcome coupling and feedback systems works in both examples?

PSG: I selected the examples because they are very different. Also, I believe the tools work. You just get different results. For example, the positive feedback loops are important in both cases, but for different reasons. In Barings, the accelerated positive feedback systems help us to understand why this system was out of control. The activities in Figure 4.2 can account for Leeson's trading activities, the bank becoming overextended in the order of $29 billion, and the eventual bankruptcy. In ValuJet, there are no noticeable positive feedback loops. There is no dynamic mechanism linking the activities of the SabreTech mechanics to the crash of Flight 592. Also, the presence of common metrics, additive forms of organizing, few intermediary outcomes, and so forth, in Barings (vs. ValuJet) means that the effects across levels should be more pronounced and easier to observe. In both Barings and ValuJet, our tools let us explain the likelihood of errors.

You: A good argument is made about different types of errors, but there is no discussion about how linkage analysis would be different for different types of errors.

PSG: You are correct. I thought that delving into this question, which is very important, would complicate this chapter greatly. However, I did try to address in a different way the importance of different types of errors. The basic idea is that different errors may interact with each other and create other errors. In Barings, I tried to point out that the errors of measurement, design, latent errors, and organizational errors were feeding on each other. This interaction among errors was an important contributor to the accelerating cycles in Barings.

Some loose interaction of errors also was present in ValuJet. It did not lead to any positive feedback cycles but probably contributed to the status quo, that is, the presence of process design and measurement errors probably reduced any corrective actions and increased the probability of an organizational error.

You: What is new in how you approach the study of organizational errors? What is the difference in your approach?

PSG: That's a great question. My answer could be another chapter! There is a lot of variation within this literature from Perrow's (1984) emphasis on technology to the complicated set of factors accounted for in Vaughan's (1996) book on the Challenger.

But let me highlight some extensions of our approach. I clearly want to add to this literature rather than just be different. Here are some points.

First, we have an explicit multilevel focus. We are looking at the intersections among the individual trader, staff, BFS, BS, BP, and external regulatory organizations. Some recent theoretical accounts of organizational errors (Weick et al., 1999), although important and provocative, do not explicitly examine the multilevel nature of organizational errors.

Second, there is a clear focus on how outcomes change in this multilevel focus, that is, we are trying to trace how changes in the trader's activities and outcomes affect other levels or units and how these units and levels drive the trader's activities and outcomes. I think both the theoretical as well as the visual mapping portrayed in Figure 4.2 is absent in many current accounts of organizational errors.

Third, there is a structured analysis. We first map the outcome coupling dimensions, such as metric similarity, to set the stage. Metric similarity and additive forms are critical in the Barings case. Then there is an explicit focus on mechanisms. For example, we say that positive feedback cycles are important. We want the analyst to look for initial conditions, the form of the accelerating cycles, and time lags. Also, we look in detail at the negative feedback mechanisms. One key in Barings is the failure of negative feedback systems to work and to explain why these mechanisms did not work. An assertion in the Weick et al. (1999) article on mindfulness is the need for vigilance in error monitoring; vigilance leads to fewer errors. However, our analysis of Barings showed there were lots of monitoring systems, but they were not used. Again, understanding the mechanisms and explaining why the negative feedback systems did not work (e.g., diffusion of responsibility, escalation) seem more promising than simply asserting the need for more vigilance.

Finally, our framing of different types of errors and the interaction among errors is another contribution. It is true that Perrow (1984) talked about the interaction among errors, but these are primarily ones on the technical system. Our discussion of organizational, design, process, and latent errors is broader and speaks to the idea that errors are more likely to be frequent than rare events.

I hope this answer helps. It is clear there is growing, useful literature on errors. The points mentioned previously represent ways that linkage analysis can extend this literature.

5 Changing Organizations:
Limiting Conditions

This chapter begins an exploration of linkage analysis and organizational change. Let me provide a brief road map. We ask the central question of this chapter: Why don't successful changes at one level affect outcomes at the organizational level? It addresses many issues underlying the productivity paradox. The chapter's focus is on observable changes at the individual and group levels and their failure to affect the larger organization. Chapter 6 starts from the organizational level and asks how organizational-level changes may affect groups or individuals and how organizational-level changes may affect higher organizational forms (e.g., corporate levels). These two chapters analyze specific outcomes across levels. Chapter 7 focuses on the interrelation among different outcomes over time in the context of a change effort.

In this chapter, we begin by exploring more generally the relation between the organizational change literature and organizational linkages. Then, we explore why successful changes at one level do not affect other units or levels. Tools from our prior analysis, plus the concept of *limiting conditions,* are introduced to examine the central question of this chapter.

The domain of organizational change has been central to organizational science since its inception. Inherent in the concept of change is the opportunity to explore existing issues on both theory and practice. A brief reflection of the change literature will evoke important theoretical contributions in the writings, such as Argyris (1985, 1990), Lawler

(1986, 1992), March (1991), Mohrman, Mohrman, Ledford, Lawler, and Cummings (1989), and Pfeffer (1994).

From the field of practice, there have been many contributors to this literature, such as Deming (1986), Beer, Eisenstat, and Spector (1990), Lawler et al. (1998), Nadler et al. (1992), Nadler et al. (1995), Mohrman et al. (1989), and Wellins, Byham, and Wilson (1991).

There is every reason to believe that organizational change will continue to be a dominant theme for organizational researchers and practitioners. In many ways, our field is reactive in nature (Goodman & Whetten, 1998), that is, what we work on is affected by changes in our environment. If we think about even the near or midterm environment, there are obviously strong environmental forces that will change how we think about organizing work. Changes in globalization of markets, new technology, political systems, and social demographics and values represent powerful forces in reshaping processes of organizing. They will sustain organizational change as a central theme in our research.

Why Focus on Linkages

A fair question is how the linkage concept can help and extend our understanding of organizational change.

Perhaps the simplest answer to this question concerns our assumptions about change and our tendency to think in terms of a specific level, that is, we create changes in an organization with a specific level focus and then make assumptions about the change process of other levels or units. The major contribution of the linkage analysis is to make these assumptions explicit. By making these assumptions explicit, we should learn more about organizational change processes.

Let me develop this point with some examples. In the mid-1970s, there were growing concerns about declines in U.S. productivity and increasing inroads from foreign competition. That environment was, in many ways, the precursor to the broad employee involvement movement that began then and has continued until today. It has taken many forms, such as team-based organizations, TQM, process reengineering, and labor-management change efforts.

Let me return to an example I mentioned previously. In 1979, I wrote a book about one of the first major system-wide interventions built around self-designing teams. The change was led by Eric Trist and Gerald Susman. I led a team assessing the process and results of the change. One distinguishing feature of the book was its interdisciplinary approach to assessing organizational change over time. The setting was coal mining. The initial unit of analysis was the self-designing team. However, given the 24-hour operation of a mine, the final unit of analysis was the three crews that made up a section.

We were able to demonstrate that this system-wide change, built around self-designing teams, led to definable, positive changes in productivity costs and safety attitudes at the section level. Note that a major focus of this project and other organizational change projects (e.g., on selection, job design, group process) was on a particular level of analysis. The assumption has often been that changes in improving one level (individual or group) undoubtedly will help the organization. I can remember one member of my team, an economist, asking if I thought these changes had a positive impact on the mine or corporation to which the mine belonged. My assumption and immediate response was "Yes." The problem with that assumption is that it may or may not be true, and it drives to the heart of what the linkage concept is all about. It asks, "Will changes in activities, events, and outcomes at one level have an effect on another level?" When I wrote the book 20 years ago, I did not ask the linkage question; I assumed the answer, and that was a mistake.

Another example concerns system-wide change in which the level focus is on the organization. In a survey of strategies for "high performance organizations," Lawler et al. (1998) provided data from a large sample of firms on the use and the impact of different strategies on organizational effectiveness indicators. That survey captured change practices coming from a variety of intellectual movements, such as employee involvement, TQM, and process reengineering. Within each of these broad categories, there is an enumeration of specific strategies. For example, within employee involvement, there are practices related to sharing information and rewards. And within these categories, there are specific change systems, such as all-salary systems, pay-for-knowledge systems, and gain sharing under the reward category.

The goal of this research is both to describe what firms are doing and the impacts of the practices on organizational effectiveness indicators. An underlying theme of this work and others is that any of these practices cannot be understood in isolation. Typically, these organization changes reflect multiple system or practice changes. For example, an employment involvement change program includes a complex set of integrated changes that lead to organizational improvements. So it is the combination of changes in information systems, knowledge reward systems, and decision-making and power systems that create effective organizational change.

The basic result from this survey (Lawler et al., 1998) is that these practices make a difference. The combination of changes such as team building, cross-training, skill-based pay systems, job enrichment, and employee participation improve performance outcome, profitability, and employee satisfaction. The assumption is that these organizational changes in training, reward systems, and power lead to complementary individual, group, unit, and, eventually, organizational-level outcome changes. But there is little, if any, evidence of testing these assumptions. We do not see how information sharing or skill enhancement leads to individual- or group-level changes, which, in turn, lead to organizational-level changes. Our goal is to show how the existing tools we have discussed plus some new ones can shed some light and insights on some of the untested assumptions in these system-level change interventions.

Another reason for exploring the linkage concept in the domain of organizational change is that it might give new lenses to explore important recurring issues. For example, over the last 10 years, there has been an increasing interest in what is called the *productivity paradox.* The basic idea behind this paradox is that there have been very large investments in information technology without any discernable improvements in productivity at the industry or firm levels (Attewell, 1994). Although the research and the controversies about these findings have been in the realm of economics, it also is a relevant issue for organizational science (Attewell, 1994). In an organizational change perspective, firms buy and implement information technology. If the implementations fail, then understanding the paradox is pretty straightforward. Failed implementation means costs were incurred and no benefits followed. But what if the implementations were successful and yet no changes occurred at organizational levels? Then, understanding the paradox is less clear. If successful changes occur at the individual level, what are the conditions when these changes will or will not appear at the organizational level? In this sense, the linkage tools should provide critical new insights into understanding organizational change as it relates to the productivity paradox.

The third rationale is that a linkage analysis may introduce some new perspectives on change. Consider the analysis of the Barings case in the last chapter. That was about a changing organization versus an organizational change intervention. A very important concept in that analysis was the role of positive feedback systems. Understanding both the initial conditions and the forces driving the accelerated cycles of behavior (see Figure 4.2) is really the essence of understanding why this 200-year-old bank went bankrupt. Explicit in this analysis is the fact that initial small changes can have long-term reverberations, nonlinearities in changes, incubation periods before positive accelerating feedback cycles begin, and so on. Although these ideas appear in writing on organizational change (March, 1991; Nadler et al., 1992; Nadler et al., 1995), our linkage analysis gives them a more central role. It is in this sense that our tools may provide new lenses to describe and analyze change.

The last rationale is that our linkage analysis may be a way to think about organizational superstitions. Organizational superstitions are strongly held organizational beliefs about the connections among objects that may not bear any correspondence with reality. Many organizational change efforts are tied to these superstitions. Let me give you an example. We were doing research in a company that was implementing many change activities to increase customer satisfaction. In our work, which was not directly related to these change activities, it was striking how many senior managers believed there was a direct link between change in customer satisfaction and profitability. This belief was strongly held, and these managers would not engage in any discussions about these two outcomes. In most of our linkage analysis so far, we have talked about changes in the same outcome across units or levels. Another important use of linkage analysis is to examine changes across outcomes over time. By examining the interrelation of outcomes over time, a task rarely undertaken in most organizational change research, we can gain better insights into when relations between outcomes (e.g., customer satisfaction and profitability) are a reality or merely an organizational superstition.

We must address a basic question in this chapter: What are some of the conditions that limit organizational changes at one level from affecting other levels? The key ideas in this question are that (a) there are

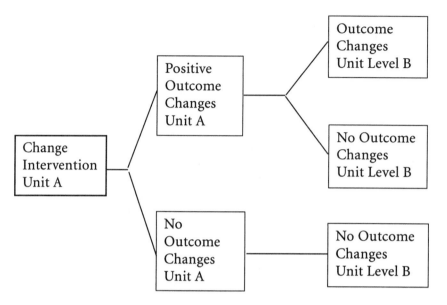

Figure 5.1. Change Interventions and Outcomes

changes in activities at one level or unit; (b) these changes lead to changes in outcomes at that level; and (c) these changes in activities, events, and outcomes at one level have no impact on outcomes at other levels or units.

Figure 5.1 describes some possible change paths. We are interested in the impacts of successful implementation in Unit A. If a change implementation at one level were not successful, we would not expect changes in other units or levels. The concept of limiting conditions focuses on why successful changes in Unit A have no impacts on other units, the focus of this chapter.

Understanding Limiting Conditions—
Prior Tools

Some of the concepts discussed in Chapters 3 and 4 address some of these limiting conditions. In our discussion of outcome coupling, there were five factors that bear on understanding why successful changes at one level do not affect other levels. Let me briefly remind you.

Dissimilarities of Metrics

The dissimilarity of metrics across levels is one factor. If the metrics are different (e.g., increasing numbers of product designs and organizational profitability), it is much more difficult to trace the impact of increased productivity of the design unit on organizational profitability.

Forms of Organizing

I described a simple typology of additive, sequential, and reciprocal forms of organizing. These are good forms with which to unfold some limiting conditions. In the additive form (e.g., coal mine), the units are relatively independent. This means that an organizational intervention, for example, to improve safety should have a direct impact on accident rates at the mine level. In sequential or reciprocal forms, changes in one unit may not create changes in any other units or organization levels unless there are significant coordinating mechanisms in operation.

Number of Intermediary Outcomes

The number of intermediary activities between outcomes at one unit or level and outcomes at another level is another limiting condition. The greater the number of intermediary activities, the greater the costs of coordination and the probabilities that internal and external factors may mitigate the effects of changes in one unit or another.

Programmed Activities

The degree that the intermediary activities are programmed or unprogrammed also addresses the question of limiting conditions. In an automobile assembly plant, there is a highly programmed sequence of activities. Operation A leads to Operation B, and so on. In computer-integrated manufacturing facilities, the interdependencies and causal ordering are very tight. There are few buffers. This means that changes in any part of the system need to be integrated simultaneously with all other parts of the system. This is a challenging and difficult task in this complex environment. Therefore, the more the intermediary tasks are programmed, the more unlikely that changes at one unit or level will affect another.

Time

The last dimension we discussed under outcome coupling was time delays. In the Barings case, losses generated by the Singapore office are immediately transferred to the parent company. Only the speed of the accounting system limits the transfer time. In other settings, there are long lead times between changes in outcomes at one level and their impact on other levels. For example, the time period from design conception of a new automobile to its "roll out" is measured in years, not days. Longer time periods permit internal and external factors to attenuate the influence of positive outcome changes (e.g., more efficient design process) earlier in the process on later outcomes.

To summarize, successful changes at one level will have a limited or no impact on other organizational levels or units when (a) the outcome metrics are different, (b) the forms of organizing are sequential or reciprocal, (c) there are many intermediary activities, (d) these intermediary activities are highly programmed, and (e) there are long time delays between the outcome changes.

Understanding Limiting Conditions— New Tools

We now turn to three other concepts that may limit changes at one level from affecting another level.

Constraints

Constraints are a particular form of limits (cf. Fine, 1998). For example, a production capacity constraint occurs when a downstream operation (manufacturing) cannot absorb the increased rate of new product designs. Or your local post office mail production facility increased the level of automation in the form of multiline optical character readers or bar code sorters, and the productivity of these operations in terms of letters sorted per hour increased. However, your "postal factory" is tied to a complex national delivery system. Unless that delivery system can absorb the increase in letters sorted by destination, the internal production units will show increases in productivity, but the "local factory" will not show increases in productivity.

There can be other types of constraints such as in the communication system. In either case, constraints in subsequent sequential or reciprocal operations create slack in the upstream operation and preclude outcome changes from affecting outcomes in units or at the organizational level (Goodman, Lerch, & Mukhopadhyay, 1994). We would look for constraints primarily in sequential or reciprocal forms of organizing or when there are many intermediary activities.

Negative Consequences

Here, positive outcome changes at one unit (e.g., product design) have *negative consequences* for other downstream units. Negative consequences often are not anticipated. Negative consequences may be generated by a variety of factors. A study by Kraut, Dumais, and Koch (1989) examined the impact of new information technology systems on customer service representatives in a utility company. The expectation was that the new systems would increase the productivity of these customer service representatives and make their job easier and more doable. The analysis of this technological implementation indicated positive improvements in the customer service representatives' job. However, an unintended consequence was that the supervisor's job became more difficult. The difficulties were manifested in more difficult problems to solve and more coordination issues. The "net effects" of this intervention then become less clear, and its impact on other units or levels is reduced.

A different example concerns how changes in units negatively affect each other. A manufacturing unit has the capacity to absorb the new product designs, but the increased number of new and different products increases the complexity of the manufacturing work, which, in turn, may increase unit costs in manufacturing, a measurable performance criterion for manufacturing, but not necessarily for product design. Another scenario is simply when the increase in new products to be manufactured increases levels of stress and tension in manufacturing. The basic idea in these examples is that changes in one unit have observable positive or beneficial impacts for individual and unit performance. However, in a sequential or reciprocal form of organizing or when there are many intermediary activities, these changes have negative or undesirable consequences for other downstream operations. The net effect may be that no observable outcome changes or even possibly negative outcome changes occur at the organizational level (manufacturing plant).

Core-Peripheral Distinction

The distinction between *core activities* and *peripheral activities* appears in a variety of organizational literatures (e.g., Scott, 1995). Core activities represent the technological and managerial activities involved in transforming inputs into outputs critical to the organization's survival. Peripheral activities are indirectly related to this transformation process. Although the distinction is somewhat arbitrary and there is some shifting of activities that were considered peripheral in traditional environments to become core, in new technological environments (Susman, 1990), the concepts can be useful for our analysis of linkages.

In my own fieldwork in organizations, I have operationalized the core-peripheral distinction by asking, "If the set of activities in question stopped, would this condition substantially impact the organization's transformation process?" Consider a computer-integrated automobile assembly plant that has a body shop, paint shop, and assembly area. If any one of these operations stops or the logistic system stops, the whole plant stops. These are core areas. In all of these plants, there are training operations that are critical to the long-term survival of the organization (Parsons, 1951). If the training activities stopped, the plant would still function in the short- and midterm because they are peripheral activities. Or let's think of a sales-service organization with offices distributed in multiple locations. If the sales or service function stopped, there would be a direct impact on sales and customer satisfaction indicators. These are core activities. However, if the training program for service people stopped or the community service activities of the office stopped, there would be no direct and immediate connection with these two performance indicators. These, then, are peripheral activities.

How does the core-peripheral distinction help us understand inhibiting conditions in the context of organizational change? Organizational changes that successfully improve outcomes in peripheral (as opposed to core) units may not be observable at other units or organizational levels. An intervention that improves outcomes of the training department may not lead to discernable changes in other units or at the organizational level.

Connections between improving outcomes of the training department and outcomes at the firm level are very complicated. Let's say that changes in training led to increasing the number of people trained per day. The question is how the training productivity indicator relates to some firm productivity indicator. The connections with organizational-level outcomes are complicated. If more people are trained, the first question is whether training leads to any changes in individual-level performance (e.g., they are more productive in their job). There is a host of factors (e.g., supervision, equipment, and reward systems) that may facilitate or inhibit the effects of training. The next question is, assuming there are individual-level performance improvements, whether these changes will affect group, unit, and organizational levels. We have had considerable discussions thus far about why changes in individual performance may not affect other units or levels. So the changes in peripheral activities, such as improving the productivity of the training department, are less likely to affect unit- or organizational-level outcomes than are changes in core activities.

How can we use these limiting conditions to deal with the central question of why successful changes at one unit or level do not affect changes in activities and outcomes at another level? First, any of the factors, such as constraints or sequential forms of organizing, can reduce the impact of successful changes in one unit on another. Each of the factors is relatively independent of the others. Constraints can exist in additive or sequential forms of organizing. Negative consequences can occur in units with larger or smaller numbers of intermediate activities.

Second, although these limiting conditions are conceptually independent, some are likely to cluster. In sequential or reciprocal forms of organizing with large numbers of programmed intermediary activities, with inherent time delays, we are probably more likely to see more constraints and unanticipated negative consequences. It is the combination of these factors, rather than their independent effects, that minimizes the impact of a successful change in outcomes in a particular level or unit on other units or levels. Some of these combinations may be more inherent (i.e., a large number of sequential intermediary activities with constraints), whereas other combinations may be more random or unique to some organizational context.

Consider the combined impact of limiting conditions in the earlier example of the customer service department in the utility company. A change intervention using information technology improved the productivity of these customer service agents. Do we expect this unit-level productivity change to affect other organizational levels? If we start with the outcome coupling tools, we know that the metrics of productivity are different between this unit and the level of the company. Also, we know that there is reciprocal independence between this unit and many other units (e.g., repair unit, billing unit) and the supervisor of this unit. If the increase in productivity in the customer service unit leads to more requests for repair or billing services, and if these units cannot absorb the increased capacity demands (i.e., constraints), we would expect no relation between customer unit changes and outcome changes at the organizational level. Also, if the increased productivity by the customer service representatives leads to a decrease in supervisor performance, as reported previously, the impact on other units or levels is reduced.

Tracing Relative Contributions in Outcomes

Here, I want to introduce a different analytical perspective that should complement our analysis of limiting conditions. Let's assume we introduce change in a core activity and there are no capacity constraints or negative consequences generated within the larger system. In this case, we want to think about how changes at one level will be discernable at another level. I introduced the term *relative contributions* because I do not think you can predict a 1-to-1 correspondence between changes across units or levels. If, for example, there is a 10% change at one level, what might be the expected change at another level? Or if there is a 10% change at one level, when might I expect these 10% or any amount of changes to be observed at another level? Some of the work by Pritchard (1992) on developing productivity measurement systems parallels the concept of relative contributions.

To explore this issue of relative contributions in terms of functionality and time, let me frame this scenario in terms of the concept of *production function*. Production function refers to the relations (degree and functionality) between the factors of production and production outcomes. In a variety of contexts, I have used this concept in evaluating the effects of organizational change.

For example, in one study (Epple, Goodman, & Fidler, 1983), we examined whether a system-wide intervention built around self-designing teams increased productivity. The setting was mining crews and their sections. A production function in this setting refers to how labor and capital (in this case, machine downtime) contributed to coal output. The implication of specifying a production function is that it indicates the relative importance of factors that affect production. It also points out the complexity of the production process.

Our job, among others, was to see if the intervention changed productivity at the group level. Simply looking at the outcome variable and determining whether it increased or decreased would lead one down the wrong intellectual path. Many factors affected production, and they were not identical across sections. We asked a different question: Did the intervention of self-designing teams shift or change the production function? For example, we found that self-designing teams, compared to traditional teams, were more productive in dangerous mining conditions. Accidents had a smaller negative effect on productivity in self-designing teams than in traditional teams. More formally, we examined changes in the coefficients in the estimated equations concerning outputs as a function of a set of input variables.

A related issue was to understand the time lags between changes in the input factors and time. For example, increasing the training for crew members may have an impact on productivity, but it probably will not be immediate. There will be a time lag between assimilating the training and applying it to improve productivity. Introducing more reliable equipment, on the other hand, may have a more immediate impact by reducing downtime and improving productivity.

Performing an assessment of change is not as simple as starting with the outcome variable and seeing whether there is a difference between $time_1$ and $time_2$. To understand how the change effort changes the production-function relation, you must first have a fine-grained understanding of the production process. Remember the earlier example that self-managing teams worked better in dangerous conditions than did regular crews. That type of insight was important in understanding why change efforts have effects. I want to extend this example from the group level of analysis to the firm level to understand how outcome changes in the group level may affect the firm's outcomes.

Suppose a change has been introduced that increases productivity in one section by 10%. Let's also assume there are three other sections and that there is a transportation system in place that moves the coal to the electric utility company, the point of creating value. Also, there is a managerial and other support subsystems (e.g., Schneider & Klein, 1994) that make the whole mine work. The story should begin to emerge. We do not expect to see a 10% increase in the firm's productivity based on the section's 10% increase in productivity, because this section is only 25% of the total production. Also, holding constraints and negative consequences constant, there are other factors of production that contribute to changes in the mine's production other than the mining sections (e.g., transportation system). Without a deep understanding of the production process, you cannot build a production function for a unit or the organization. In specifying the production function, we need to make rough estimates on relative contribution of factors as well as functional form (i.e., linear or nonlinear forms). If we can do this exercise, we will be better able to know *a priori*, given changes at one level, what to expect in terms of outcome changes at another level.

I can spin out a similar exercise with the manufacturing plant example mentioned previously. Suppose a new CAD system was introduced that increased design productivity at the individual and department levels. Here, the situation would be more complicated because the outcomes are dissimilar, the form of organizing is sequential, there are many intermediary programmed activities, and so on. The question is, did changes in activities, events, and outcomes at the design department level change the value of manufactured goods at the plant level? The task remains the same. What is the production function for predicting the value of goods manufactured at the plant level? In part, the value of goods will be related to the number of new products designed. Also, it will be affected by the manufacturing and logistics subsystems, as well as by the managerial and other support subsystems. What we want to know is what is the relative contribution of the number of new products designed to the value of goods manufactured in light of the other factors of production? If we know that, it will be easier to understand the potential contribution of a 10% increase in new products designed to the value of goods manufactured. For example, we estimated the production function for this firm and determined that the number of new products was a relatively low contributor to variation in the value of goods manufactured. In this situation, it will be very difficult to trace changes in outputs from the design unit to the outputs at the firm level.

Concluding Thoughts

- Our focus has been on conditions that limit successful changes in one level or unit from affecting outcomes at other units or levels.
- I reviewed some earlier concepts, such as forms of organizing and number of intermediary activities. These tools are part of the prior analysis. They highlight the relative difficulty in tracing outcomes across levels or units. For example, if the outcome metrics are different across units, it will be more difficult to trace changes across units. These tools also indicate conditions (e.g., reciprocal forms, many intermediary events, and time delays) when outcomes across levels will not be highly correlated.
- The appearance of constraints, negative consequences, and the focus in peripheral areas will further limit changes in one level from affecting outcomes in other levels.
- Estimating the relative contributions of outcomes using a production function approach represents another level of explanation for why changes in one level may not be observed at other levels. Here, we want to estimate conceptually or empirically the (a) relative contribution of a particular outcome at one level (number of new product designs) to some outcome at another level (value of goods produced), and (b) time relation between these outcomes. This exercise provides heuristics to trace changes in outcomes across levels.

Conversation Five

You: In discussing limiting conditions, there was no discussion on failed implementations. Is that not a primary reason for the productivity paradox?

PSG: Your observation is very important. The implementation process is key to any successful change. I agree it is one approach to explaining the productivity paradox. Firms invest lots of money in new information technology, the technology is poorly implemented, and there is no value produced by the investment. But I think the real paradox occurs when, for example, a new technology is successfully implemented in a unit and produces positive outcomes, yet there are no benefits at the organizational level. That is a much harder problem.

In this chapter, I wanted to explore why that happens, hence, the limiting conditions.

You: Let me frame my question in a different way. Where is the added value of the limiting condition perspective you have articulated to the broader literature on organizational change?

PSG: I think one fundamental contribution of this perspective is framing a different question. The driving question in most organizational change research ultimately deals with what are the critical processes for explaining successful or unsuccessful change? My perspective differs, first, in that I am interested in a multiple level or unit view of change. I want to examine a different question: Why do successful changes at one level or unit have no impact on positive outcomes at the organization level? It is clear that many organizational interventions are based on the premise that successful changes and outcomes at one level will lead to positive organizational-level changes, but this premise is assumed, and it may not be true. A second contribution of this chapter is the identification of the limiting conditions and the concept of relative contribution. The process of conceptually or methodologically understanding the relative contribution of changes at one level or unit on the organization is unexplored in the change literature.

You: You seem to treat dimensions of limiting conditions as independent factors. Aren't they related?

PSG: I see factors such as forms of organizing or constraints as independent tools for analysis. Clearly, there are interrelations. Constraints are more likely to be important in sequential rather than additive forms of organizing. But my goal is to provide some tools and let you use them in a way that provides insights on why successful changes in some units do not affect other units. I would begin with the outcome coupling concept and then move to constraints, negative consequences, and the core-peripheral dimensions.

You: The production function idea seems quite useful, but I doubt it has practical value. Few organizational researchers are likely to build large production databases to ask these questions.

PSG: Your observation is consistent with a lot of assessments of change. But remember, the main ideas are (a) to get the researchers or change agents, who are focusing on a particular unit of analysis (e.g., group), to also think about impacts on other units of analysis (e.g., organizational), and (b) to try to estimate the relative contributions of changes at the level they are working on to other units or organizational levels. One could do this using a panel of experts or by building a data set. The work by Pritchard (1992) indicated, for instance, that expert ratings can be used to get this type of data. The key idea is to become sensitive to the need for estimating relative contributions.

6 Focusing on
System-Wide Changes

In Chapter 5, we explored why changes at one unit or level may not have impacts at other levels. The focus has been on why individual, group, or unit changes may not affect organizational-level outcomes. A number of tools have been introduced to understand these linkages.

Let's take a different approach and look at system-wide versus unit-level change (Lawler, 1986, 1992). The new question is: What are the conditions when system-wide changes have (or do not have) positive effects on individual-, group-, and corporate-level outcomes? *System-wide changes* refer to changes in a large number of subsystems and their elements, versus one subsystem or unit. These subsystems include (a) technical subsystems, which are defined by elements such as layout, processes, supplies, and equipment; (b) organizational subsystems, which are defined by elements such as communication, decision making, authority, socialization, and reward mechanisms; (c) human systems, which are defined by abilities, skills, and values of organizational members; and (d) social subsystems, which are defined by elements such as norms, informal arrangements, and culture, as well as other subsystems dealing with external and internal adaptations.

Two different cases are presented here. One deals with system-wide change at the organizational unit level, in this case an automobile factory, and the implications of these changes for individuals, groups, and the factory. The second deals with system-wide changes at the corporate level. This case focuses on the relation between changes at the factory or staff units on the corporate level.

Table 6.1   Characteristics of Lean and Mass Production Systems

Lean Production Systems	Mass Production Systems
General purpose, multifunctional automated technology	Highly specialized equipment and jobs
Complex, multivendor equipment	Less-complex technology
Short production runs, different products	Long production runs
Highly interdependent system	Moderate interdependence
No buffers	Buffers
Downtime immediately stops system	Downtime effects moderated by buffers
No repair areas	Repair areas

SOURCE: From "Individual and Organizational Productivity: Linkages and Processes," by P. S. Goodman, F. J. Lerch, and T. Mukhopadhyay, 1994, in D. H. Harris (Ed.), *Organizational Linkages: Understanding the Productivity Paradox* (p. 67), Washington, DC: National Academy Press. Reprinted with permission.

System-Wide Changes— Organizational Unit

To illustrate organizational unit changes, I want to explore the work on lean production systems. I selected lean production systems because they represent system-wide changes at the organization level and because there are some good empirical studies in this area. This research is best exemplified by the work of MacDuffie and his associates (MacDuffie, 1995; MacDuffie & Pil, 1997). They collected data on a large sample at automobile assembly plants all over the world, and there are measures of inputs (e.g., level of automation and organizational arrangements) and outputs (e.g., vehicles produced per unit of time). There are obviously variations among the plants in terms of their overall effectiveness, measured in economic and human terms. Our interest is to use these systems to illustrate linkage analysis.

Table 6.1 contrasts the lean manufacturing systems to the traditional mass production system created many years ago by Henry Ford. The words, perhaps, do not indicate the substantial differences between these two manufacturing systems. Consider the following: I was in one of these lean plants, and car seats from an outside supplier were late by

Table 6.2 Technical and Social Characteristics of High-Performance Lean
Production Systems

Technical Systems	Social Systems
General purpose, multifunctional automated technology	**Organizational Systems**
Complex, multivendor equipment	Fewer job classifications
Short production runs, different products	Fewer status differences
Highly interdependent system	Problem-solving teams reactive
No buffers	Problem-solving teams proactive
Downtime immediately stops system	Rewards systems at individual, group, and organizational levels
No repair areas	**Human Systems**
	Multiskilled workers
	Intensive training in problem solving

less than an hour. The whole plant shut down. You should note that the seats were scheduled to arrive 1 hour before they were to be used and in the order they were to be used. This is a very interdependent and fragile system. Other features of lean manufacturing systems include shorter production runs, which means that this interdependent system needs to be flexible. More complex automated technology means that solving downtime problems will be more difficult than in traditional manufacturing systems, but one cannot afford to have downtime because of the interdependent nature of lean production systems.

Table 6.2 presents the features of this technical lean production system coupled with a particular organizational system that leads to high performance.

There are some empirical findings (MacDuffie, 1995; MacDuffie & Pil, 1997) that lean production systems, when coupled with work systems—including teams and problem-solving groups—and human resource practices—including contingent compensation, lower status differentiation, and greater training—contribute to greater productivity and to some extent greater quality levels. There is some evidence that the combination of the lean production system, work systems, and human resource practices had a greater impact on productivity than would have been predicted by the addition of these individual components. This finding speaks to the impact of the congruency between technical and social systems. *Congruency* refers to the fit or complementarity between components in the technical and social system (Trist, Higgins, Murray, & Pollock, 1963).

What's missing from this interesting set of studies on lean production systems are the data on individual- or group-level outcomes, that is, there is documentation of these system-wide changes and the plant-level effects, but we do not have direct evidence on changes in outcomes at the individual or group levels. This absence of data speaks to the reason for writing this book. Researchers tend to focus on levels and not on the linkages among levels.

There is, however, some indirect evidence from the high-commitment research literature that changes must be occurring at the individual and group levels. The social system features in Table 6.2 mirror many of the characteristics (e.g., multiskilled workers, team-based) of high-commitment work systems. From a variety of different types of organizations, using various research methodologies, there is evidence these system-level changes increase worker commitment (Lawler et al., 1998), group performance (Walton, 1987), and reduce absenteeism (Zager & Rosow, 1982). It is probably fair to assume these changes are going on in our case on lean production systems. Let's assume these technical and organizational system-level changes have changed activities, events, and outcomes at all levels of analysis. The question still remains: How do we account for these results? I want to suggest two ways to answer this question.

The first answer and the most traditional is to evoke the socio-technology argument, which basically argues for joint optimization of social and technical systems (Trist et al., 1963). Stated another way, congruency between technical and social features will improve organizational effectiveness. Let's look at an example to highlight this concept of congruency.

A few years ago, I was with some people at a robotic paint shop in a lean production plant. Something happened to one of the robotic painters and one of the booths shut down, which sharply reduced production. Robotic paint shops are complicated technological systems requiring different types of expertise. This particular plant had many different job classifications within the plant and within maintenance, that is, production and maintenance job activities are separate, and within maintenance there are many different jobs. The consequence was that the production worker had to wait for the maintenance worker, who in turn had to request other types of maintenance workers to get the job done. By contrast, in a lean production setting with a multiskilled, fewer job classification social environment, the response time is much faster and the coordination costs are substantially lower. The multiskilled worker solves the problem rather than wait for others. In this setting, there is a match between the complex and tightly coupled technical and social system. Responsiveness to downtime is a critical factor in highly interdependent systems such as lean production systems.

This sociotechnical perspective has been a very useful way to think about the effectiveness of alternative work setting arrangements. In my own work, I have found it to be a useful way to develop a first-order understanding of work settings. One limitation of this perspective is that the concept of congruency is not clearly defined (cf. Van de Ven & Drazin, 1985). Another is that it seems more useful in *ex post* explanation. For me, the next important concern is that it does not capture the dynamic processes and interrelations going on in these lean production systems. It does not capture the interplay among levels. How do changes in individual- or team-level performance affect the organization? How do the system-level changes modify the activities and outcomes of groups?

Linkage Analysis

Let's return to our linkage tools and apply them to the high-performance lean production place. The relevant social system is the plant and its network of suppliers. The suppliers are critical because of the no-buffer policy and "just-in-time" nature of the inventory system. The relevant time period for analysis should be from the birth of the lean production systems. Unfortunately, most of the data on lean production systems are cross-sectional. Also, a prime focus has been on the plants and not on the supply chain (for an exception, see MacDuffie & Pil, 1997).

The concept of *outcome coupling* is relevant in our analysis. First, the outcomes have some similarity, but they vary across operations. In the body shop, one counts parts and completed bodies per hour. The paint shop and assembly operations also count vehicles per hour, but obviously, the nature of the vehicles is different (i.e., one is a painted vehicle body, the other is a completed vehicle). When we talk about quality in the body shop or paint shop, the outcomes are more dissimilar. Second, the *form of organizing* is sequential. The principal operations are the creation of the body, the painting of that body, and assembly and testing of the vehicle; the basic sequence is fixed. Third, in terms of *intermediary operations,* there are many complex activities and outcomes between the creation of the body and the completed vehicle. Fourth, the activities are fairly *programmed,* that is, the sequence of operations is fairly fixed. The last dimension is *time.* On one hand, time is affected by the number and complexity of intermediary operations. On the other hand, this is a time-focused industry. The principal metrics in the plants are vehicles per hour. For most assembly plants, the time a vehicle remains in the plant from beginning to end is measured in hours or a few days. Therefore, the time period is relatively short.

What does the picture look like (see Figure 6.1)? This is a sequential form of organizing. The description of outcome coupling pointed to the large number of programmed intermediary operations, which increases the difficulty in tracing linkages across units and in finding changes in outcomes between the units and the plant. All the inhibitors to effective change (e.g., constraints, negative consequences) that we identified in Chapter 5 should be relevant here. Despite these difficulties, we have evidence that this combination of technical and social features in Table 6.2 works in terms of higher productivity and quality. Also, there is some indirect evidence that there are positive changes going on at the individual and group level (i.e., in terms of commitment and performance) that are contributing to overall plant performance.

How do we account for these results? On one hand, we have a system-wide change that is leading to unit and level changes in activities and outcomes, which are contributing to overall plant outcomes. On the other hand, our mapping of the organizational environment in terms of outcome metric dissimilarity, sequential organizing with many intermediary activities, and other limiting conditions suggests that this is an environment in which impacts of unit changes on organizational outcomes might not be readily observed. We think there is a set of com-

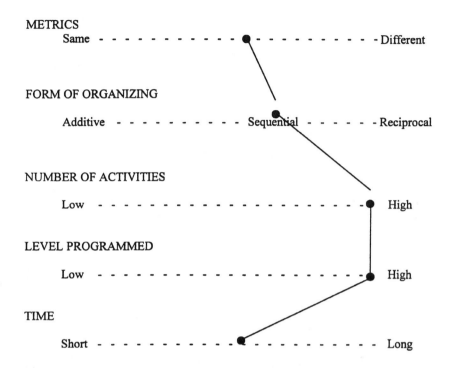

Figure 6.1. Dimensions of Outcome Coupling—An Auto Assembly Plant

pensatory processes underlying the structural components of lean systems. These processes facilitate the linkage of activities and outcomes among different units and levels and account for the higher performance. These four processes are coupled with our earlier discussion of negative and positive feedback systems.

Reactive and Proactive Problem Solving

An important component of lean production systems is the presence of fast-response, highly trained problem-solving teams. The goal of these teams is to minimize any disruption to the system. In even the best of systems, there will be poor parts, machine breakdowns, and miscommunication. Interruption to any part of this highly interdependent system can bring the whole system to a halt. Therefore, the

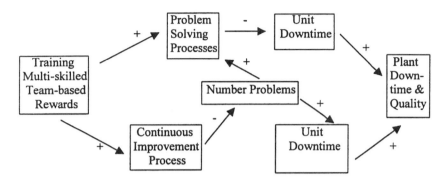

Figure 6.2. Problem Solving and Continuous Improvement Processes

capability of a fast, effective response to a problem is critical to the operation of these plants. This characterization fits our earlier description of negative feedback systems. Discrepancies between desire and actual states in lean production systems must be resolved, hence, the role of the fast-response problem-solving teams.

Another team-based problem-solving process in this environment focuses on continuous improvement. In many ways, the job of these teams is to improve processes that will eliminate production problems and improve quality. The better the continuous process teams perform, the fewer the problems for the problem-solving teams.

Figure 6.2 describes the role of these two processes and their interrelation. The development of effective problem-solving processes should reduce unit downtime. Because this is a highly interdependent production process, downtime in a unit will lead directly to system downtime. Therefore, there is a direct connection between changes in activities and outcomes (e.g., downtime) in a unit and those at the plant level.

Similarly, continuous improvement teams improve the production processes in a way so as to eliminate recurrent problems (e.g., downtime) in a unit, which, in turn, will reduce plant downtime directly. These two processes are both independent and interdependent. This interdependence comes in the form of positive feedback loops. Consider the following scenario: Process improvements reduce the number of recurring problems. As the number of recurring problems drops, the problem-solving teams will be less distracted and more able to focus faster and solve more quickly any problems. Quicker resolution of downtime problems reduces organizational downtime and increases productivity.

Another scenario is that as the number of production problems decreases, there may be less need for problem-solving teams. One option is to switch the problem-solving teams into continuous improvement teams. In this case, more continuous-improvement teams lead to more process improvements in outcomes such as downtime.

To summarize this argument, I am suggesting that effective lean production systems have two key processes—reactive problem solving and continuous improvement. Independently, these two processes lead to reductions in unit downtime, which directly translates into plant-wide downtime in this production environment. Both processes are directed to eliminate the gap between actual and desired behavior (the negative feedback process). At the same time, there are positive feedback processes between problem solving and continuous-improvement teams. Improvements in the production processes can change the role of the problem-solving teams, which, over time, can enhance the continuous improvement process.

The reader should note that the previous examples have focused on the outcome—downtime. The reason is that the metric of downtime is the same across units in the plant and at the plant level, and there is a direct connection in this environment between unit downtime and plant downtime. In linkage terms, the effects at the unit level should be directly observable at the plant level. If I had used examples of problem solving or continuous improvement for quality, then the analysis would be the same, but the changes of outcomes at the unit and plant level would be less correlated. For example, if either problem-solving process had improved the dimensional quality of the body shop production, the impact on plant quality levels would be less direct and more difficult to discern. The dimensional quality of an auto body is not the same metric as the quality of a completed vehicle. Also, there are many intermediary activities that affect the overall quality of the vehicle. Stated in another way, poor dimensional quality will make the assembly operations more difficult (i.e., the part does not fit) and create more quality errors. However, good dimensional quality does not directly lead to high vehicle quality.

I want to push this analysis further by arguing that there are some other underlying compensatory processes that explain why the technical and organizational features of lean production systems in Table 6.2

lead to high performance at the individual, group, and plant levels. These processes facilitate the linkage of activities and outcomes at different levels. They represent a finer-grained analysis than simply evoking the concept of congruency. The other three processes are described subsequently.

Multiple Coordination Processes

There are multiple *coordinating mechanisms* operating at different levels and across levels in the high-performance plants. Some coordination is by plan, in which elaborate computer-integrated manufacturing systems manage outside and inside work flow. Other coordination is by feedback, in which real-time information systems permit immediate adjustment by external (e.g., vendors) or internal personnel. Some coordination mechanisms focus on system-wide coordination, whereas other systems are decentralized to provide operators immediate information to manage specific production activities. An alternative way to build coordination is to reduce the need for coordination. The movement in these plants to fewer job classifications is a way to reduce coordination costs. These multiple, different, and overlapping mechanisms contribute to linkages across levels, that is, given an environment (e.g., sequential organizing, large number of intermediate activities, highly programmed) that inhibits changes at one level from affecting other units or levels, the multiple overlapping coordinating mechanisms provide an offsetting or compensatory force to facilitate changes across units and levels.

Focus of Attention

Focus refers to the activities and outcomes to which people pay attention. Employees in the body shop may focus on their specific job activities or the activities and outcomes of the body shop. Or they may focus also on overall outcomes of the plant. The more there is a common focus or shared mental model at different levels among all employees, the more likely individual activities and energies will lead to changes in group or unit activities and outcomes that link to activities and outcomes at the plant level. There were a number of factors building a common focus of attention in these high-performing plants. Extensive training about one's job as well as the larger system contributes to this shared focus. A contingent reward system that links project to individual and plant performance focuses people's attention on multiple levels of analysis. Focusing attention on multiple levels is key to linkages across levels.

Motivation/Commitment

High-performance systems require high levels of *energy and commitment.* These need to be distributed throughout the work area rather than in one work department. Some of the factors enhancing energy levels include moving to multiple skill jobs, greater responsibility for problem solving, and contingent reward systems. In any case, high levels of energy distributed horizontally and vertically and commitment to analysis and the larger organization are necessary for correlated changes across levels. This is particularly important because lean production systems can be more stressful than traditional production environments due to the high levels of interdependence. One operation can shut down all others.

Although we have presented the processes independently, it is only their joint effect that will explain high performance in lean systems and correlated changes across level of outcomes. If there is a well-designed coordination system with commitment only at the individual level, it is unlikely this combination will lead to high performance. Similarly, if the workforce is focused on and highly committed to their own jobs or their own groups, it is unlikely in this interdependent system that one change at the one level will affect other levels.

So what is the formula? We want to create a system in which these processes are (a) self-reinforcing, and (b) facilitating correlated changes across levels (see Figure 6.3).

Consider the following scenario: Multiple coordination mechanisms strengthen coordination across the plants, which eliminates bottlenecks and stress. The contingent reward system and training get this energy or commitment focused at individual, group, and organizational performance. If workers are committed to improvements at the individual, group, and organizational levels, there is less likely to be suboptimization (Cyert & March, 1963), and coordination activities horizontally and vertically will be strengthened. Better coordination of activities should reinforce the multiple-level focus of attention and minimize stress, which could detract from high commitment levels.

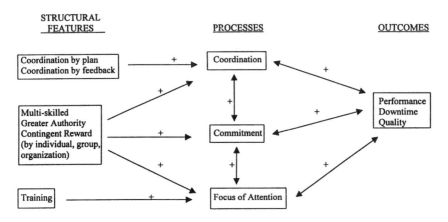

Figure 6.3. Coordination, Commitment, and Focus of Attention

If these three processes are self-reinforcing (a form of positive feedback), there should be performance consequences. Let's visualize some possible synergies. A highly committed workforce in the body shop solves a tooling problem that will have downstream consequences for the assembly area. Two things occur. The outcomes (dimensional quality) of the body shop improve and the changes are communicated to the assembly area (coordination), which can initiate some new practices, which respond to the changes in dimensional quality. In this case, changes in outcomes in one unit are likely to be correlated with outcomes in another unit, which should affect overall quality. Improvements in overall quality should promote greater commitment, which, in turn, should reinitiate this set of activities.

Summary

Let's conclude this analysis with the following observations. Creating correlated change in outcomes across multiple levels is a difficult and challenging task when the organizational setting is characterized by sequential operations and many intermediary operations that are programmed. In addition, these lean systems are very fragile. Many possible events (e.g., downtime, parts shortage), although located in one part of the plant, can, in a very short time, affect the total operation of the system. Yet, we have some evidence that some combinations of technical and social components of lean production systems yield high individual, group, and organizational performance. Many of the limiting conditions in Chapter 5 seem to be offset.

I introduced the two problem-solving processes to indicate that fast response to resolve problems that threaten the system, as well as improvement of the fundamental processes to eliminate problems, are key elements of effective lean production.

The reinforcing nature of the reactive problem-solving and continuous-improvement processes, depicted in Figure 6.2, suggests one reason why changes (e.g., in downtime) at one level may lead to changes at the plant level. The positive feedback cycles among the processes and outcomes are an important part of the analysis.

The three processes—coordination, focus of attention, and commitment—were identified to articulate the connection between unit changes and organizational changes. The three processes together played a critical role in the earlier example I presented about problem-solving changes that improved dimensional quality in the body shop. The focus of attention was not solely on unit improvements, but on downstream consequences. The commitment and subsequent coordination activities to enable downstream operations to benefit from the upstream changes were critical. Stated another way, these three interacting processes bridge changes in one unit to complement changes in other units and levels. This bridging is key to why these systems work (see Figure 6.3).

System-Wide Changes—
Corporate Level

I want to explore a second case on system-wide change. The social system for linkage analysis is the interrelation between an organizational unit and the corporation. It has two important features. First, it permits us to look at the relation between plant and unit (e.g., staff) changes on corporate-level changes. Second, the particular change evolved over a 10-year period. The prior case focused at the plant level, and the design was cross-sectional, not longitudinal. Looking at system-wide change over time provides another vantage point.

The setting for this case is a 10-year change at Champion International, a large producer of paper products. These events are captured in a new book, *What Works: A Decade of Change at Champion International,* by Ault et al. (1998). The underlying orientation of this change process is similar to our examination of the lean production system. There is a strong sociotechnical orientation coupled with elements of high-performance/high-commitment systems found in the writings of Walton (1987), Lawler et al. (1998), Nadler et al. (1992), and Nadler et al. (1995).

Before we can examine some linkage issues, I need to give you a sense of what happened at Champion International. This is only a brief picture. I encourage you to read the book for a thoughtful account of corporate-level change process. We can think about change at Champion International at the plant or unit level and at the corporate level. Plants are the major units producing value along with corporate or staff units such as accounting. At Champion International, the change starts in the mid-1980s in two plants—one a greenfield site, another an existing facility. Then, it extends throughout the whole organization. We can examine (a) how change occurs at a given plant and the results of these changes over time, (b) the diffusion of these changes to other plants or units, and (c) the results of these plant-level changes over time to the corporate level.

Effective plant or unit change in their book is organized around three concepts—*clear alignment, strong capabilities,* and *letting go.* Clear alignment means that the organizational change effort, business strategy, values, and core technology are congruent or aligned. Strong capabilities means that competence, commitment, and cooperation have been significantly increased. Letting go means providing optimum latitude or empowerment.

Table 6.3 summarizes the managerial levers used to create change at the plant or unit level. A brief scan of this table indicates that this is a major comprehensive change effort. All systems are being changed. A lot of the change is being initiated at the plant level. That means the job design or gain sharing activities are individualized to each plant as opposed to being the same across the company. Some of the change elements reside at the corporate level. These include the role of the top leadership and the philosophy of the change process, to parts of the training system.

What you cannot see in the table is that this is a sustained change effort. External shocks in the form of market downturns were met with persistent focus on the change philosophy and behaviors that supported this long-term change process. Examples would be continued investment in plant and people, even when there were substantial drops in revenue as a function of market conditions.

Let's look at some snapshots of Table 6.3 at the intersection of the rows and columns. Creating alignment among the change strategy, competitive strategy, values, and core technology is a complicated task. A key word in the prior sentence was "among." That means all four components need to evolve in a similar direction. Creating this alignment comes from leadership style and a corporate transition team at one level to intensive off-site sessions and training. If a strong customer focus is part of the competitive strategy, then structural redesign such as organizing staff departments around customers or artifacts such as "floating" customer-driven quality banners are part of creating alignment. Similarly, if one wants to create and enhance capabilities in competence, reward systems can play an important role. Pay for skills can increase competence. Gain sharing programs can enhance levels of cooperation. Or one could turn to job redesign or goal setting as a way to increase commitment. Let me invite you to move along the rows and columns in Table 6.3 to see if you can explain other intersections. The basic idea is that plant or unit changes are comprehensive and sustained. Also, as we mentioned in the lean production case, these changes are congruent, that is, changes in operating structure, rewards, and participation mechanisms are congruent with each other and with the technical and market systems.

We can move from the plant or unit level to the next question: How were sustainable change processes created over the whole operation? There are multiple plants in different locations producing different products as well as different corporate units. Table 6.4 captures the change process over time, beginning with the startup to the diffusion and institutionalization processes. It begins with the initial change process in the two plants—Quinnesec and Pensacola. Then, there is a multiple strategy diffusion that ranges from structural mechanisms, such as the transition team and consultants, to training, visits, and conferences as other mechanisms used to diffuse the understandings, values, and artifacts of the change. The institutionalization process captured a variety of structural changes, ranging from a very large capital investment program to new reward systems and organizational redesign. I think the diffusion process is a critical part of this story. However, our focus is more on thinking about this change in linkage terms. I

Table 6.3   Managerial Levers Used to Create Alignment, Build Capability, and
            "Let Go" of Direct Control

Managerial Levers	To Create Alignment	To Build Capability	To Let Go
Job and structure redesign			
Mills	X	X	
Accounting	X		
Corporate technology	X		
Interfunctional teams	X	X	
Management information systems			X
Top management			
Corporate structure	X	X	X
Rewards	X	X	
Pay for skills		X	
Gain sharing	X	X	
Something extra	X	X	
Bonuses		X	
Recognition		X	
Participation mechanisms			
Off-site sessions	X		X
Teams	X	X	X
Goal setting, planning, and information policies			
Targeting	X	X	
Open books management	X		
Human resource policies			
Training and education	X	X	X
Selection			X
Appraisal			X
Employment security		X	
Union-management initiatives			
Fostering tactics		X	
Forcing tactics		X	
UPIC-Champion forum		X	
Joint statement of principles		X	

Table 6.3   *Continued*

Managerial Levers	To Create Alignment	To Build Capability	To Let Go
Best practices initiatives			X
Leadership style			X
Project management	X		
Change-process structures			
Transition team	X		X
Lead consultant	X		
Internal organizational-development staffing and training	X		X
Language: Banners for change	X		
"Participative Management"	X		
"Redesign"	X		
"Customer-Driven Quality"	X		

SOURCE: From *What Works: A Decade of Change at Champion International* (pp. 46-47), by R. Ault, R. Walton, and M. Childers, 1998, San Francisco: Jossey-Bass. Reprinted with permission.

want to move on, but again I invite the change enthusiasts to uncover what's behind the words in Table 6.4.

What were the results of this elaborate change process? At the corporate level, there were a number of indicators. There was a 47% increase in productivity (tons/employee) during the 1986-1990 period. Costs increased less than the industry average, and overhead was considerably less than the industry benchmark. There were clear improvements in quality, and Champion earned a variety of awards for quality excellence from customers. Other external recognition as "company of the year" from the paper industry's magazine was received during that time. The authors of *What Works* (Ault et al., 1998) noted that these corporate-level changes were attributed to substantial improvements in 5 of 11 pulp and paper plants, and moderate changes in 2 to 3 of its other plants. In addition to the plants, there were changes for five corporate support staff groups, such as applied technology and control/accounting.

Table 6.4 Champion's Change Process

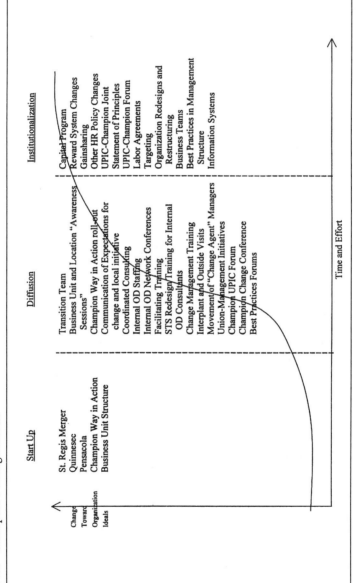

	Start Up	Diffusion	Institutionalization
Change Toward Organization Ideals	St. Regis Merger Quinnesec Pensacola Champion Way in Action Business Unit Structure	Transition Team Business Unit and Location "Awareness Sessions" Champion Way in Action roll-out Communication of Expectations for change and local initiative Coordinated Consulting Internal OD Staffing Internal OD Network Conferences Facilitating Training STS Redesign Training for Internal OD Consultants Change Management Training Interplant and Outside Visits Movement/of "Change Agent" Managers Union-Management Initiatives Champion UPIC Forum Champion Change Conference Best Practices Forums	Capital Program Reward System Changes Gainsharing Other HR Policy Changes UPIC-Champion Joint Statement of Principles UPIC-Champion Forum Labor Agreements Targeting Organization Redesigns and Restructuring Business Teams Best Practices in Management Structure Information Systems

Time and Effort

SOURCE: From *What Works: A Decade of Change at Champion International* (p. 25), by R. Ault, R. Walton, and M. Childers, 1998, San Francisco: Jossey-Bass. Reprinted with permission.

Outcomes of the changes within the plant at the individual or group level are more difficult to document in terms of quantitative indicators, that is, there is no systemic survey of data about indicators such as work attitudes over time. However, throughout the book, there is information indicating that there were changes at the individual and group levels. Consider the following indicators: At the plants, jobs redesigned ranged from 30% to 80% per plant. In general, the literature on job redesign points to improvements in job attitudes, motivation, and quality (Hackman & Oldham, 1980). The American Society of Training and Development cited Champion and the union for "outstanding improvement in employee involvement." Other research on successful employee involvement programs (Lawler et al., 1998) indicates that there are positive attitudes and motivation with work. The union-management contract was extended from the typical 3-year contract to a 5-year contract. Extension of contract time is likely to be related to greater feelings of trust and positive attitudes toward the company. The injury rate dropped by nearly two thirds, substantially better than the industry average. All of these indicators, plus research on high-commitment systems, provide some evidence that there were changes at the individual and group levels.

Now that the setup is complete, I want to explore linkage analysis of this change. The principle question is, How do activities, events, and outcomes at the plant or unit level affect outcomes at the corporate level? A second possible question is, How do system-wide changes at the plant level affect individual, group, and organizational levels? This second question has been examined in our discussion of lean production systems and is not the subject of this analysis.

Let's focus on how changes in activities, events, and outcomes at the plant affect corporate-level outcomes.

In terms of outcome coupling, the *outcome metrics* of productivity at the plant and corporate level—ton/employee—are the same. The plants are additive *forms of organizing*, there are few *intermediary connections*, and there should be few delays between changes in plant productivity and corporate indicators. Therefore, changes at the plant level should be highly correlated with corporate-level changes.

There are no obvious *limiting conditions* between the plants and the corporate level in terms of outcomes such as productivity. The plants clearly represent the core components of this company.

A plant's *functional contribution* to the corporate-level productivity will help determine the expected linkages. For example, whether a plant contributes 10% or 1% of total productivity will determine our ability to assess the impact of changes at the plant level on any corporate-level changes. In the former case, it will be easier to trace impacts of changes from the plant level to the corporate level. We have used productivity language to discuss these changes. Other outcome variables—such as costs, delivery time, and quality—would be treated the same way.

The analysis tools are the same when we switch to other organizational units, but the results are somewhat different. The system-wide change was directed to corporate support groups as well as the plants. For illustration purposes, let's take the accounting unit, which we will assume is at the corporate level.

In terms of outcome coupling, the *metrics* for productivity in a corporate staff unit are quite different from the central productivity of a paper company—tons/employee. This unit is likely to illustrate a *reciprocal form of organizing.* Orders come in, they move to scheduling, plants deliver products for which they are billed, and then the financial transaction is completed when funds are received. There are many *intermediary activities* between improvements in productivity of the accounting unit and corporate-level productivity, that is, the relation between changes in the support departments processing accounts payable and corporate productivity indicators is, at best, indirect, and the *time delay* is hard to determine. These factors substantially reduce the connection among outcome indicators between these levels.

In terms of *limiting conditions,* problems of constraints and negative consequences are more likely in context with reciprocal independence and multiple chains of activities. *The functional contribution analysis* also would be relevant, that is, what is the relation between productivity of the accounting unit and corporate-level productivity (measured in terms of total tons or tons per employee)? I think the answer to that question is "very little." That does not mean this support function is unimportant. Rather, in the case of productivity, the accounting group is not a core contributor. There is no direct or substantial relation between improvements in the accounting department productivity and corporate-level productivity.

Let's change the outcome variable to customer satisfaction. Now the answer will change. The ability of the accounting group to receive and process billing in a responsive way is one important attribute of customer satisfaction (Schneider & Bowen, 1995). We need, then, to assess the relative contribution of the accounting customer activities on overall customer satisfaction. In most customer satisfaction surveys, there are factors such as speed and accuracy in responding to inquiries, quality of billing procedures, and so on. The analysis would look at total satisfaction as a function of these factors and factors outside the control accounting group (e.g., satisfaction with the product). If we can determine the relative contribution of this corporate support group to total customer satisfaction, we can better assess how increases in customer satisfaction created by the control/accounting group will relate to changes at the corporate level in overall customer satisfaction. By changing the outcome variable from productivity per ton at the firm level to overall customer satisfaction, the linkage between outcomes at the support group and corporate level changes.

Our analysis has indicated that there are different linkage arrangements between the plants, staff units, and the corporate level, and these arrangements vary to some extent based on the outcome under investigation. Now, I want to end this chapter on a more speculative note and ask whether the combination of productivity changes at the plant level affect corporate-level indicators greater than do the individual contributions of the plants (I want to leave out the support departments for this exploration).

Previously, I suggested there should be some fairly direct linkages between the plants and corporate levels for the following reasons:

- Metrics, in terms of productivity, are the same for plants and the corporate level.
- The plants are additive forms of organizing.
- There are very few or no intermediate activities between plant productivity and corporate productivity.
- There is little time delay between changes across levels.

My closing question is whether there is some interaction among the plants and/or between the plants and corporate level that leads to higher corporate-level productivity than we would have predicted by considering the productivity of each plant in isolation. Do some of the facilitating processes we have identified previously play a role in the plant-corporate linkage?

Unfortunately, there is no empirical data to assess whether there are some synergistic effects among the plants and/or between the plants and corporate. However, some of the underlying processes we have identified previously in this chapter may contribute to such an effect.

Focus of Attention

The focus-of-attention mechanisms are at both the corporate and plant level. Consider this comment from a middle manager at a mill: "Our new paper machine must perform not only for the financial success of this mill but as a symbol of what our organization and our office is all about."

That is a powerful statement. It indicates that this individual is focusing on the plant and the corporate level and understands some of the important organizational symbols and culture. The organizational culture at Champion includes strong beliefs and values about the customer, quality, continuous improvement, and empowerment. The statement is not one about suboptimizing at the plant level to the detriment of the organization as a whole. If the focus indicated in the previous quotation characterizes the orientation of other people and plants at Champion, then perhaps the contribution of the plants together is greater than if we simply aggregated the productivity measures of the plants in isolation. In an earlier discussion (see Table 6.4), we enumerated a set of factors—such as senior leadership, transition committee, extensive training, and reward system—that contributes to focusing employees both at plant and corporate levels on a common corporate strategy, corporate culture, and set of outcomes.

Commitment

Another question is whether commitment and energy levels of the plant are driven by the plant-level changes, or whether the corporate-level changes are a source of commitment and energy for the plants, that is, the interaction between plant and corporate changes leads to higher levels of commitment and motivation than we would find by looking only at individual plants. I want to argue for the latter case for the following reasons. First, the development of a common culture has both a focus-of-attention function and a motivating function. Adopting values about customers and quality drives behavior. Second, during the

10-year change period, there were significant external shocks in the form of poor market conditions that could have derailed the change effort. Instead, corporate management continued a significant capital improvement campaign and invested in training. In this market context, these are powerful signals about the importance of the change effort and the articulated organizational values. In addition, the signals should build organizational loyalty and commitment. If this analysis is correct, then changes at the corporate level should lead to greater levels of commitment than we might expect from looking only at commitment levels generated by each plant.

Problem Solving

The problem-solving processes we discussed previously may have played a role in the augmentation of the change, that is, when changes at particular plants were slower than expected, some corporate-level problem solving may have been initiated to stimulate the change. Greater diffusion can stimulate commitment both within and between plants.

There were a variety of mechanisms for knowledge sharing, a form of problem solving. Although plants were permitted to individualize the changes to their own context and environment, knowledge sharing among the plants about pitfalls or best practices might have accelerated the learning curves during the change process. This interaction among these relatively independent plants is one argument for expecting that changes at the corporate level would be greater than the individual contribution of all of the plants. (Note: I left out the coordination mechanisms because I wanted to signal a situation in which the change activities were customized according to the unique features of each plant rather than a centralized change effort.)

The basic argument that these processes may have led to outcome changes between plant and corporate level in an order of magnitude greater than we may have predicted from focusing on each plant in isolation may be visually portrayed. Figure 6.4 captures the initial part of the corporate change process. A few plants were involved. Initiations from the corporation in the form of symbols, resources, and rewards launched the change process at the plant level. Given the complexities of the change elements (see Figure 6.3) and the strategy of individualizing the change at the plant level, the design and implementation phases

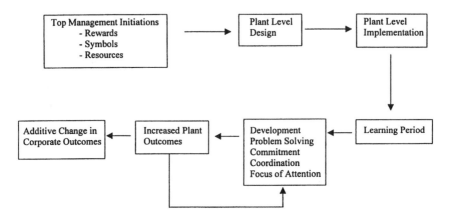

Figure 6.4. First-Level Changes Between Plants and Corporate

required high levels of commitment, but any performance changes at the plants probably lagged behind these activities. Over time, the development and interaction among the problem solving, commitment, and focus of attention moved the plant to a state in which outcomes at one level (e.g., group) positively affected activities and outcomes at different levels (e.g., individual and plant), and performance outcomes across levels noticeably increased. The performance success at the individual, group, and organizational levels fed back to accelerate the interaction among the processes and then to improvements in plant performance and some additive changes at the corporate level.

The second level of change (see Figure 6.5) appears when the number of plants initiating system changes and experiencing performance improvements increased. The increasing number of plants leads to a new form of a community. Instead of focusing solely on one's own plant, there is a sense of a community of plants going through similar experiences. The community becomes a shared understanding through a variety of forces. First, the presence of others creates some shared awareness. Communications from the corporate leadership, sharing learning experiences among the plants, and support for the change effort during an economic downturn all contribute to the creation of this community. The experiences of the change and the positive outcomes create a condition for sharing some common beliefs and values among these plants.

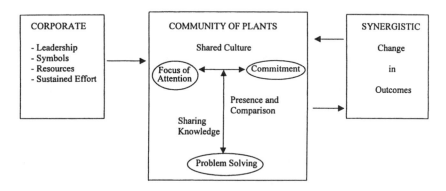

Figure 6.5. Mapping Synergistic Linkages Between Plants and Corporate

The consequences of the community for each of the plants may be the following: The presence of other plants increases the level of commitment both to the plant and the corporation. Suboptimization practices are less likely. The culture enhances commitment levels and focus of attention to the plant and corporation. Knowledge sharing is more likely under these conditions and should improve problem-solving processes at the plant level. The intersection of knowledge sharing, commitment, and focus of attention should enhance productivity and quality levels of the plants beyond what the plants would have contributed on their own.

Concluding Thoughts

- Our focus has been on two examples of total system change that have led to positive organizational outcomes. The assumption is that there were corollary changes at the individual, group, and department levels, and at plant and corporate levels.

- A problem with typical research on change is that we have a level bias. If changes occur at the system level, we assume these changes should have positive effects on other units or levels. This assumption is never tested or explained. In the two cases we examined, we could infer changes at other levels, but they are not systematically examined.

- One theoretical explanation underlying both cases is a congruency model. Congruency among technical, organization, and social systems leads to high performance. A problem is that the meaning of congruency, how to measure it, and how to make *ex ante* predictions about congruency are not well delineated.

- We have demonstrated that the outcome coupling concept is key to any linkage analysis. In our discussion of the lean production process, downtime was isomorphic between the unit and the plants. Reductions in downtime from reactive or proactive problem solving at the unit level should be directly correlated with changes at the plant level.

- In the condition in which the outcomes are different or there are many intermediary activities, the impacts of changes at one level on another are more difficult to realize. I argued for compensatory mechanisms. These mechanisms come in the form of the interaction among coordination, commitment, problem-solving, and focus-of-attention processes. The correlation between unit and plant outcome changes can be strengthened by these processes and their interactions.

- In discussing the second case, I pointed to how the linkage analysis changed if we were focusing on plant versus support group impacts on corporate productivity. Similarly, I showed how changing the outcome measure from productivity to customer satisfaction had different implications for tracing linkages. The key lies in the dimensions of outcome coupling, such as metric similarity.

- In the discussion between changes at the plant level and corporate level, I raised a different question. Instead of asking whether plant-level outcome changes lead to corporate-level outcome change, I asked whether the combination of plants interacting with the corporate level contributed at a level greater than their individual contributions. The key idea was a "community of plants," and the processes discussed previously may lead to changes that are more synergistic in nature, that is, changes at the plant levels were amplified in the plant-corporation interrelations.

Conversation Six

You: I liked the movement in this analysis of change from a unit level to plant level to corporate level. But as the number of chapters increases, so do the explanatory concepts.

PSG: Let me tell you how I keep the analysis structure simple. I think there are four boxes of tools—outcome coupling, limiting conditions, feedback systems, and the compensatory process mechanisms. I always start with the first two boxes. Outcome coupling and limiting conditions really lay out the chart in detail. These tools are good in explaining where navigation across levels will be easier or more difficult. The feedback systems and process tool kits are helpful in explaining why changes in one level affect other units or levels, particularly in situations in which navigation is more difficult. I also don't think you need to use all the tools in each of the boxes.

You: Okay, but show me where is the intellectual yield from using these tools in the change context. Please be specific.

PSG: The tone I have tried to develop in this book is positive in nature. I think the linkage issue opens up a whole new area of research and thinking. I have not tried to build my arguments by criticizing others.

But let me respond to your question and use the book by Ault et al. (1998) as an example. I could have used other current books on organizational change.

A central concept in their conceptualization of change is creating alignment among the change, business strategy, core values, and technology. I think this is a useful concept, but very general in nature. It represents a form of "congruency thinking" that is very common in the organization literature. But as I argued in the beginning of this chapter, the concept is too general. What does alignment mean? How do I know when alignment occurs or how much alignment occurs? At one level, this concept can help us organize our thinking, but at other intellectual levels—developing propositions, understanding basic underlying processes, directing measurement strategies—it is not very helpful.

If you look at Table 6.3, there is a long list of levers that might create alignment. What is missing is that we do not know how these levers work. What are the mechanisms by which alignment occurs, and how does this affect unit-, plant-, or corporate-level outcomes? Implicit in this list of levers is the assumption that these changes will create individual-, group-, unit-, and plant-level changes. However, how these complementary changes occur is not well examined. It is left to our imagination. But we know that establishing this linkage across units and levels is difficult.

Let me be more specific about our tools and their contribution. First, the outcome coupling dimensions and the corollary limiting conditions indicate that the paper plants will be difficult settings in which to create multiple level/unit changes. These are sequential forms of organizing with programmed intermediary areas. Indeed, in their book, Ault et al. (1998) reported that substantial changes occurred in some of the plants and not in others. Unfortunately, we do not have detailed information on the plants that did not change. In a linkage analysis, I would have looked immediately for the compensatory process mechanisms (e.g., coordination, focus of attention) to explain the differences between the plants. Our prediction is that without the presence and synergy among the process mechanisms, no plant-wide improvement will occur.

Second, the outcome coupling dimensions and the concept of relative contribution can help us understand the relation between staff-, unit-, and plant-level changes on corporate-level changes. When I analyzed the linkage between plant- and staff-level changes on corporate changes, I could generate propositions about the linkages by varying outcome similarity and the number of intermediary activities. A focus on understanding the linkage of plant and staff unit performance with corporate performance is all but absent in the organizational change literature.

Third, I think we need to move from merely listing relevant concepts to being more specific about their dynamic interrelations. Figure 6.2 captures the relation between reactive problem solving and continuous-improvement problem solving. The key idea is not that these are independent processes. Rather, they are portrayed using the concept of positive feedback loops to show their dynamic interrelation. I would argue that both the substantive processes (e.g., reactive problem solving) and the way they are portrayed (via positive feedback loops) is a more comprehensive, analytic way to understand change than is simply listing variables (e.g., see Table 6.2). I encourage change researchers to think about cross-level effects, explain cross-level effects, and measure and analyze these effects. The tool box is a way to think about and explain cross-level phenomena.

You: The examples you selected in this chapter seem to be very traditional forms of organizations. Even if lean manufacturing systems are a newer evolutionary form, they are still discrete manufacturing systems. It is not clear how your analysis would work with newer forms of organizing, such as virtual teams.

PSG: I accept that observation as an interesting challenge. I wanted to ground my analysis in real organizations. Also, if there were data available, that would be more attractive. For example, one very attractive feature of MacDuffie and his associates' work on lean manufacturing (MacDuffie, 1995; MacDuffie & Pil, 1997; Pil & MacDuffie, 1996) is that they have a large worldwide database on automobile plants, with input and criteria data. That is quite unusual in organizational studies.

But, let me respond directly to your comment with an example. We are doing a new study on knowledge sharing in a knowledge creating organization that is organized around offices worldwide. The major manufacturing occurs in people's heads. Work is highly professional, diverse, semistructured, and done in teams. There is no production technology as we saw in the previous two examples. I think this is a very different environment, but I could use the tools of linkage analysis. For example, if new information technology were introduced to enhance project team performance, I would still use the outcome coupling and limiting conditions concepts to set up the analysis. Then I would use the processes, for example, to trace effects from teams to the offices and to the corporate entity. In Chapter 8 on learning, I develop such an example.

You: Most of your analysis uses anecdotal data. There is no hard data.

PSG: You are quite correct. But in one sense, that is the point in the book. Critical data have not been gathered regarding linkages and their effects. If people study lean production settings, I want them to think about the linkage concept and collect data across levels and try to trace effects. Even if this were done initially in a qualitative way, I am sure it would help their own research and shed more light on this question.

7 Change and Linkages
Among a System
of Outcomes

The focus of this chapter is on organizational change and linkages among a system of outcomes. In our prior discussions on change (Chapter 5), we examined why successful changes at some levels are not evident at other levels. The productivity paradox marked that discussion. In that analysis, we tended to focus on one outcome (e.g., productivity) at a time. We moved, then, to an analysis of system-wide changes at the plant level and at the plant-corporate levels. The underlying question of how changes at one level are reflected at other levels or units remained the same. Again, the focus was on single outcomes, such as tons per employee or customer satisfaction. Now, I want to explore linkages among a system of outcomes that are affected by organizational change interventions. The emphasis is more on the interrelations among outcomes over time than on the change process itself (Hall, 1976). We move from tracing whether changes and subsequent outcomes from one level appear at another level to tracing how changes in outcomes are interrelated over time. For example, let's assume an intervention at the group level leads to changes in outcomes (e.g., productivity, quality, and costs) that are linked to organizational-level changes in these outcomes. In this analysis, we focus on the changes among these outcomes over time.

Tools for Analysis

In this analysis, I use some of the tools presented in prior chapters. The concepts of positive and negative feedback cycles, as well as delays and nonlinearities among variables, are important for this analysis. Because these have been used in previous chapters, they are not elaborated here.

These concepts have been central to a line of research on organizational change led by a group of researchers in the "systems of dynamics" tradition from MIT (Repenning, 1997; Sterman, 1994; Sterman et al., 1997). I note this group because I have found its research very compelling. Also, although this research group seems conversant with some of the traditional organizational literature on change, the reverse is not true. Their work and approach often are not reflected in the current organizational change literature.

I find some of the features of their work compelling and relevant for linkage analysis:

- A focus on positive as well as negative feedback cycles
- A focus on delays and nonlinearity in the relations among variables
- A multiple methodology strategy, which includes mathematical specification of variables, relations, organizational simulations, extensive diagramming of systems or relations, and collecting actual data
- An examination of change in the context of practical problems, such as the implementation and success of TQM efforts

A Case—Analog Devices Inc.

To examine organization change, linkages, and the system of outcomes, I make extensive use of a case on Analog Devices reported by Sterman et al. (1997). I draw heavily on this case because it does a nice job tracing the interrelations of outcomes over time. If you want to learn more about the detailed analyses, go to that article and Repenning (1997).

Analog Devices produces integrated circuits and systems. It has been a very successful and well-regarded company. However, in the early 1980s, it missed a number of important objectives, and one strategy was to introduce a TQM change effort. The specifics of this system-

wide change are not necessary for our discussion. All of the TQM principles (e.g., customer focus, continuous improvement), practices (e.g.,
problem-solving teams), and methods (e.g., Pareto charts, Ishikawa di-
agrams) were part of this change effort. Extensive training, a quality office, and many other features found in moving successful TQM programs were also part of this change effort. Newer concepts, such as the
"balanced score card" (Kaplan & Norton, 1996) and a new methodology for estimating quality targets also were put in place.

From the implementation of the change in 1987 to 1989, there were
significant reductions in defects and production cycle time, and other
indicators such as yield and on-time delivery significantly increased.
Indicators such as product development time did not change. In terms
of economic indicators, operating income (price minus cost of goods
sold and indirect costs) was declining.

In 1990, Analog Devices found itself in a crisis situation, stimulated
by a recession, with falling operating income and stock price. The first
layoff in the company's history was initiated, and jobs were transferred
to locations outside the United States. A major strategic refocusing
took place in which products and distributors were changed, and a major acquisition took place. Because of these events, there was a movement away from TQM activities, and outcome measures such as defect
measures and on-time delivery either remained the same or got worse.

An Analysis

Previously, I said the case is really for illustrative purposes. I want to focus on the time prior to the financial crisis in 1990 and on the paradox
of organizational change improvements. How can improvements (e.g.,
lower defects) attributed to change efforts yield unintended negative
consequences and undermine the change effort itself?

I want to do this analysis by showing you some pictures. The pictures could have been taken at Analog Devices or other similar organizations.

Let's start with an initial mapping of classes of variables relevant for
understanding the change. Figure 7.1 shows the major variables, such as
the market conditions and top management strategies, that were part of
the initiation of the TQM program. Following our discussion in the last
two chapters, successful system-wide TQM changes should affect levels

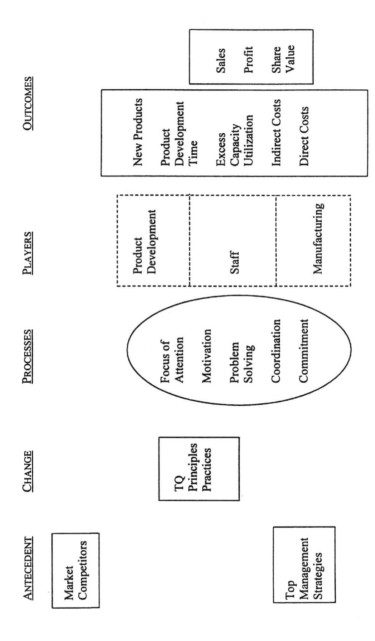

Figure 7.1. Basic Elements

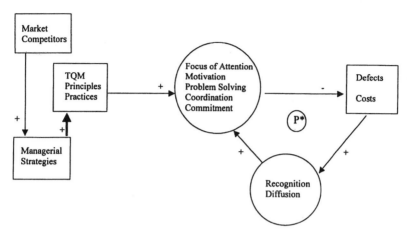

* P = Positive Feedback Cycle

Figure 7.2. Change in Manufacturing—Stage 1

of coordination, commitment, problem solving, motivation, and focus of attention, which are played out in different parts of the organization (e.g., product development, manufacturing), with the intended goal of improving different outcome variables. I have divided outcomes into those affected primarily by internal factors (e.g., defects, new products) and those influenced by external factors (e.g., sales, share value). Also, the first set of outcomes (e.g., new products) contributes to the second tier of outcomes (e.g., sales).

Figure 7.2 gives us a picture of manufacturing at an early stage in TQM. Employees in manufacturing are trained, some become committed, and the initial focus is improving quality (or reducing defects). I am separating TQM in manufacturing and in product development because they are different settings in which the lead times for changes and outcomes are quite different (Sitkin et al., 1994; Sterman et al., 1997). The relatively lower levels of complexity—technical and organizational—in manufacturing suggest that observable outcomes from TQM may materialize in a shorter time than in product development.

Figure 7.2 indicates that a major push from top management leads to the unfolding of a TQM system-wide change that increases the focus,

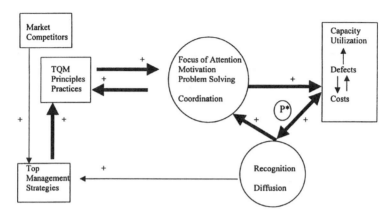

* P = Positive Feedback Cycle

Figure 7.3. Change in Manufacturing—Stage 2

motivation, and problem solving on defects. The early wins are publicized to the other employees in manufacturing, which increases recognition and diffusion of TQM, which, in turn, enhances the driving processes (e.g., motivation). The "P" symbol indicates that this system of variables has a positive feedback cycle, which, by definition, will be self-reinforcing. More recognition leads to more motivation, which leads to lower defects and successful cost reductions, which, in turn, lead to higher recognition. The thickness of the lines indicates the degree of correlation between the variables, that is, increases in motivation or problem solving are associated with lower defects and more cost reductions, but the association is not as strong as is portrayed in the management strategy-TQM relation. In Stage 1, the forces driving the change are external.

The last and important point is that the outcomes are relatively independent. Although defects and costs are associated, they are not tied together in Stage 1. There are initial reductions in defects, but these were "low-hanging fruit."

In Stage 2 (1 or 2 years into the change), the TQM effort is accelerating, more people are involved, principles and practices are becoming institutionalized, and deeper results are observable (Figure 7.3). The

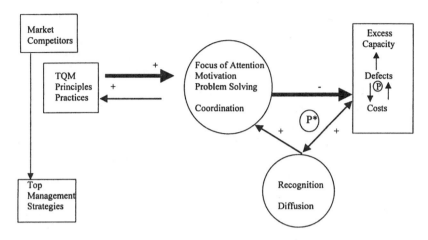

* P = Positive Feedback Cycles

Figure 7.4. Change in Manufacturing—Stage 3+

relations are becoming stronger. The positive feedback cycle (processes, outcomes, recognition/diffusion) is accelerating. Successes in manufacturing are drawing more resources from top management (and away from other areas). Increases in processes (e.g., problem solving) are fed back and modify the change effort itself, that is, increases in problem-solving skills are applied to improving the TQM process itself, which, in turn, accelerates changes in the processes and outcomes. Costs and defects are both targeted in the change effort. Also, these outcome changes are mutually reinforcing. Reduction in significant defects reduces costs. Cost reduction can simplify operations and thus reduce opportunities for defects. A positive feedback cycle is being initiated. Also, decreasing costs and defects can create greater production capacity for other products. This is probably a lagged relation in which reduction in defects and costs must reach a point before there is a change in production capacity.

Stage 3 (see Figure 7.4) presents a different story 2 or 3 years into the TQM effort. The change is established throughout manufacturing. Everyone is participating. Therefore, one of the earlier accelerating cycles has slowed considerably or come to a halt. This was the cycle in which outcome improvements were publicized, which motivated more employees to become involved in TQM activities, which, in turn, led to more outcome improvements, and so on. This positive feedback cycle decelerates as the number of employees participating in TQM moves toward 100%. Also, the effects of recognition, which in the beginning of the program were quite powerful, are now diminishing. Recognition early in the change was new and distinctive.

Because the principles and practices are well institutionalized, there is still focus, motivation, and problem solving to improve outcomes. However, there are probably diminishing returns to reducing defects and costs. In the initial years, we would expect the quality teams to attack tractable and high-yield areas. As solutions are implemented, the teams must move to less tractable problems. This means that although there is energy to solve problems, more effort must be allocated to more complex problems, and the delay between working on a problem and measuring the results will take longer (Dean & Goodman, 1993). At this stage in the process, with the change well under way, top management is likely to focus their attention on other issues, hence the break between top management and the TQM effort. In the case of Analog Devices, the recession provided a powerful stimulus for changing top management's focus from TQM to major strategic decisions to survive in the declining economic environment.

In terms of outcomes, the cost-defect outcome relation still has a positive feedback cycle, but the rate of change between the two outcomes has slowed down because of diminishing returns for new quality problem-solving efforts. By this time, the decrease in costs and defects should have generated excess production capacity.

Figure 7.5 shifts us to the product development group at Stage 1. In this unit, new products and reduction of the product development cycle are key. The simple story in this figure is that top management supports TQM activities in this area, but this is a much more complex area to apply the practices and methods. The consequences are that (a) it will be more difficult to get people motivated to work in this area, (b) there are likely to be more delays between problem solving and observable results, and (c) the quick hits and subsequent recognition are absent in Stage 1, although the processes eventually could affect product development time.

Figure 7.6 captures Stage 2 (1 to 2 years from initiation) in the product development group. Two important events are occurring. Although top management still supports the TQM program in product

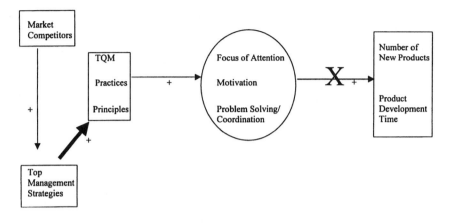

X = Barriers between the process mechanisms and the outcome

Figure 7.5. Product Development—Stage 1

development, its support has decreased. This occurred because both the early successes in manufacturing and the diffusion of the change within manufacturing redirected resources to manufacturing. The dilemma is that given the structure of product development, that function needs relatively more resources and more time than manufacturing to generate similar successful outcomes, yet they will receive relatively fewer resources.

The second critical event is that delays in improving outcomes (e.g., creating new products or reducing product development time) are likely to sharpen the discrepancy between what those employees using TQM tools were told to expect and the actual benefits. In most change activities, there may be an initial discrepancy between the promised or expected benefits and actual benefits (Sproull & Hofmeister, 1986). In most change activities, committed employees will tolerate the discrepancy until actual benefits accrue. In this context in which delays between activities and outcomes are likely to be long, the discrepancy will be more salient. This should lower the motivation to engage in problem-solving activities, that is, failure to create new products or to reduce product development time will increase the discrepancy between expected and actual benefits from investing in TQM activities and consequently reduce the process behaviors. This negative feedback cycle

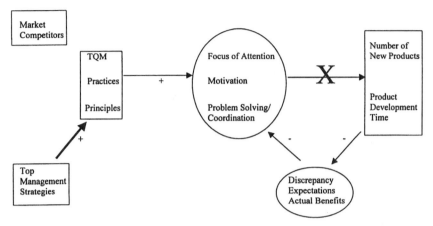

X = Barriers between the process mechanisms and the outcome

Figure 7.6. Product Development—Stage 2

should reduce the probability either of lowering product development time or of creating new products in the future. The greater the discrepancy between goals (create new products) and actual experiences, the more likely the goals will be revised downward. Consequently, no changes in activities or outcomes are likely to occur.

Figure 7.7 is really about the interrelations among outcomes. The variable "TQM Principles and Practices" is included because it reminds us of the focus of this chapter. A system-wide change process was implemented. There were teams of people in specific departments that reduced defects or costs. The consequential nature of these changes appears at the organizational level in metrics, such as defects per parts per million products. The accumulation of these department-level changes was observable at the organizational level. Figure 7.7 takes us on a different path—exploring the interrelations among outcomes. This analysis is primarily at the organizational level. Let's walk through this figure, remembering our prior analysis.

1. As the change effort unfolded, primarily in manufacturing, defects and direct costs were part of a slowly accelerating positive feedback loop. By Stage 2, reductions in defects decreased unit costs, and direct improvements in manufacturing costs removed opportunities for defects. As we moved into Stage 3, issues of di-

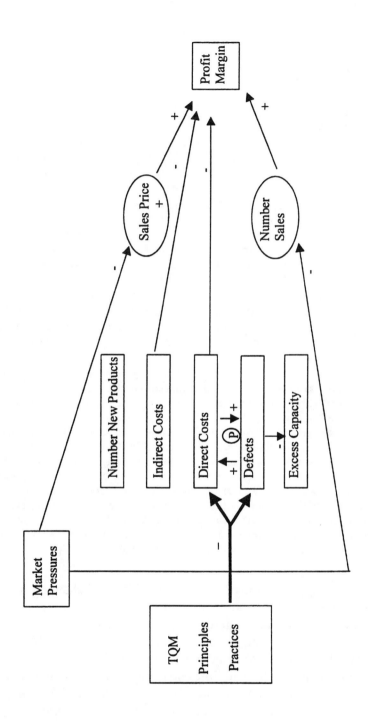

Figure 7.7. Outcome Analysis

135

minishing returns (opportunities to reduce costs/defects) slowed the rate of cost and defect reduction as well as their reciprocal influence on each other.

The improvements in costs and defects should create excess production capacity. Although we do not know the functional relations between defects and excess capacity or the particular time lag involved, it is likely that excess capacity was being created by improvements in quality and costs.

2. Improvements in quality and costs should lead to a more competitive sales price and the greater unit sales. Moreover, excess capacity creates an opportunity to create more products, which should enhance unit sales.

3. One of the characteristics of TQM programs is that they were well diffused in particular industries. As Sterman et al. (1997) argued, the quality benefits experienced by Analog Devices were being matched by their competitors. This means that any relation between better quality and increase in units sold was offset by the reduction in defects generated by competitors. There was no comparative advantage for any of the competitors in the quality-sales relation.

4. Another way to increase unit sales is through new products. The TQM initiative had created excess capacity, a necessary condition to launch new products. However, our analysis of the product development area indicated no major improvements in reducing time to market for new products. The consequence was no increases in sales.

5. The unintended consequences of the TQM improvements appear in the cost indicators. As I already reported, direct unit costs declined; however, indirect costs did not decline at the same rate, and these costs became a larger proportion of total costs. Indirect costs deal with areas such as marketing, sales, and logistics. These areas, relative to manufacturing, have higher levels of complexity. They are similar to product development in the sense that TQM efforts often do not have immediate and visible benefits. The problem at Analog Devices is that they set prices, as do other firms, by applying a markup percentage to unit production costs. Prior to the TQM effort, this markup was sufficient to cover direct and indirect costs plus a reasonable profit margin. As unit costs began to drop at a faster rate than indirect costs, the pricing (markup) policy did not generate gross margins to cover indirect costs sufficiently, and operating income at Analog Devices dropped 45% (comparing a 1985 base year to 1989).

Let's do a quick summary of the organizational change improvement paradox. TQM activities lead to improvements in quality and cost indicators in the manufacturing group and department levels. Opportunities for increasing sales and operating income were offset by (a) competitors' use of TQM principles and practices and (b) inability to reduce product development time and generate new products. This inability was attributed to the inherent difficulties in creating changes in the product development domain and, in part, to reallocating resources from this area to manufacturing, where success was more visible. Although reducing direct unit costs is clearly a positive outcome, the pricing policy that relied on declining unit costs no longer generated sufficient revenue to cover indirect costs, and profit margins fell.

One of the advantages of creating organizational simulations is that it permits asking "policy" questions. Sterman et al. (1997) asked whether Analog Devices would have been better off without TQM. The basic answer is no. Competitors would have improved their quality and costs. The simulation results show revenues falling 80% from the 1985 base level, stock prices dropping, and so on. The authors concluded that without TQM, the company would have left the industry or been taken over.

Another interesting question posed in the simulation was whether a no-layoff policy would have been a better strategy. Although we have not focused on the layoff and subsequent events, it is relatively clear that layoffs (particularly the first-ever layoff) may have undermined commitment to the TQM efforts. The interesting result is that a no-layoff policy would have little short-run effects on some of the outcomes we have been discussing. The critical point is that the relation between defects, direct costs, indirect costs, and profit margins were already in place prior to the layoffs. Maintaining job security does not change the relations among these variables. Indirect costs because of the change effort are becoming a larger share of total costs independent of the layoff policy.

The last question concerns the markup policy: Why not increase the markup to cover indirect costs and create a reasonable profit margin? The results of the simulation show that a revised markup policy improves operating profits and share price.

A logical inference, then, may be that if Analog Devices had used a more "appropriate" markup policy, the TQM outcomes might have moved in a similar direction, and there would be no organizational change improvement paradox. I do not think that this is the message one wants to take away. First, increasing prices in a declining economy is a complicated strategy, with many unexpected consequences. Second, changing the pricing policy may look good *ex post,* but organizations are not omniscient systems constantly discounting and revising traditional decision processes. Finally, my point is broader than the specifics of the case. The goal is to illustrate the complicated linkages among outcomes in a system-wide change.

Concluding Thoughts

- Examining the connections among outcomes complements our earlier analysis of how changes in activities and outcomes at one level may or may not affect outcomes at other levels.
- Development of maps (e.g., Figures 7.2 to 7.7) of the relevant relations creates a basis for deeper insights. Only by creating multiple representations can you develop insights about the relations among outcomes.
- The concepts of positive and negative feedback cycles, delays, and nonlinearities aid in the mapping process. Simply looking for static relations among variables will not work.
- Within the content of this chapter, there appear to be a number of paradoxes or dilemmas that also can contribute to our understanding of linkages and change.
  - The *organizational change improvement paradox*. This points to how expected benefits of change (e.g., reduced defects) can lead to unanticipated negative outcomes (loss in operating income).
  - The *diminishing returns dilemma*. A successful change program, over time, eventually will bring the system to a point at which it is difficult to extract any more gains that, in turn, can hurt the change effort, that is, the change effort has focused on areas in which there have been quick results, visible results, or where the tools and the problems nicely match each other. Further investments in the current system will have very low yields. As the system approaches this point, many of the positive feedback cycles that have been driving the change will slow down, and the delay between work and outcomes will increase, to the detriment of the change effort.
  - The *work context dilemma*. Rates of change will vary by work context (e.g., product development vs. manufacturing). One dilemma is that the areas with greater rates of changes will attract more resources, which, in turn, will slow the rate in other areas to the detriment of the total change effort. However, because of the lag effects, the effect on the total system will not be evident.

Conversation Seven

You: In our last conversation, you said there were four boxes of tools—outcome coupling, the feedback sections, limiting conditions, and the processes—but you only used some of the tools in this chapter.

PSG: That's true, but remember, the focus is different. I am not examining impacts of changes across levels. I could have. If I wanted to examine the impacts of the TQM intervention, I would have used all the tools. But my goal was to focus on the interrelations of outcomes over time, a different but important topic. In this case, I used primarily the processes (e.g., focus of attention, commitment) and the feedback cycles.

You:　Wasn't the simple solution in the Analog case just to ramp up new production introductions?

PSG:　Well, they clearly would have helped, given the excess production capacity. But remember, there are some important underlying points, quite independent of any solution:

- First, it is hard to understand the lag or time period between initiating successful changes and realizing benefits from these changes.

- Second, we do not have good models in theory or practice to understand the interplay between multiple outcomes over time. Chapter 7 is really about sensitizing all of us, both to recognize and to begin mapping out these relations.

You:　You seem to advocate this mapping process. I am not sure that if I read the chapter independent of the figures whether I could draw the same figures. Is this mapping process reproducible?

PSG:　At one level, there are no boundaries to this mapping process. At another level, I did define a problem space and a specific case. I wanted to trace outcomes over time in a TQM intervention in two basic areas—product development and manufacturing. Also, I listed the outcomes and the basic intellectual tools (e.g., positive and negative feedback cycles) that I wanted to use. Although there may be some variation between your maps and mine, we still have to account for the relation among defects, costs, capacity, and profitability. If there is variation in maps, the process of reconciliation would be an excellent way to sharpen our understanding of the interrelations among the outcome variables.

You:　There is an extensive literature about organizational effectiveness (Cameron & Whetten, 1983; Meyer & Gupta, 1994) that shows that organizational effectiveness indicators are not highly correlated. Isn't that one of the basic ideas in this chapter?

PSG:　Perhaps at some level, but that is not the point of the chapter. Simply showing with cross-sectional or longitudinal data that organizational effectiveness indicators are not related is not particularly informative. That "finding" has been in the literature for many years. We need to understand in a theoretical and fine-grained way why these relations unfold, lag, and change over time. We need to get inside the black box.

Meyer and Gupta (1994) presented a provocative article, at the institutional level, about the rise and fall of certain effectiveness indicators. Our focus has been at a different level—the organization. We want to understand and to predict how organizational change affects a dynamic system of outcomes in different units and in levels over time. Why does the organizational change improvement paradox occur? The Analog Devices case was a unique context. How general is the paradox? What are the factors that are likely to contribute to this paradox? In examining the diminishing return dilemma, we noted that many change efforts focus on areas in which there can be quite visible results, but, over time, there are diminishing returns from these areas, which, in turn, can undermine the change activities. Similarly, we noted the work context dilemma, which indicates that rates of change may be more rapid and visible in some work areas than in others. The dilemma is that the areas prone to more rapid changes attract more resources to the detriment of the total change effort.

I think that both using the tools and mapping the relations (see Figures 7.1 to 7.7) in various organizational change settings will provide a basis to resolve these questions and dilemmas. These are very different issues from whether organizational effectiveness indicators are correlated.

8 Organizational Learning

This chapter applies the tools for organizational linkage analysis to the area of organizational learning. Although there has been interest in organizational learning for more than 20 years (Argyris & Schon, 1978), it has clearly come to the center stage of organizational research in the 1990s (Miner & Mezias, 1996; Sitkin, Sutcliffe, & Weick, 1998; Weick & Westley, 1996). The presence of a growing number of empirical studies makes it an attractive area for exploring organizational linkage questions. It also is an area in which I have been doing empirical research over the last 5 or 6 years, and there have been some central questions that have puzzled me and others with whom I have worked (Goodman & Darr, 1998; Goodman & Olivera, 1998; Olivera & Goodman, 1998). So this chapter provides an opportunity to explore the connection between the linkage concepts and research issues in organizational learning.

This analysis has a research question: What are the impacts of learning and outcomes at one level on the activities and outcomes at different units or levels? This is the fundamental question in the book, but not the typical question in organizational learning research. Although it may not be the question most organizational learning researchers are working on, it is an interesting, important, and complementary question.

Let me give you an example of a learning situation in which the distinction between the previous research question and an organizational learning research question come into play. We have a large company with many operating units performing the same operations. The units sell and service office equipment. The units are located in different cities and operate as independent units. However, because they work with the same products, it is likely that innovations (e.g., new applications for enhanced revenue) or solutions to problems (e.g., procedures for servicing a machine) discovered in one office may be relevant for another office. Therefore, sharing knowledge across these offices may be beneficial to the individual office and the larger company, that is, learning from others will improve office and company performance. Although there appear to be obvious benefits from this form of learning, there are a lot of inhibitors (Goodman & Darr, 1998). There are motivational reasons why people in one office will not share or will not ask another office for help. Also, some kinds of problems and solutions, specifically those that are high in complexity and tacit knowledge, are difficult to exchange.

Later in the chapter, I develop an example of knowledge sharing in distributed environments using the organizational linkage tools. Here, my interest is to sharpen the difference between these two research questions:

1. Organizational learning question: What are the factors that influence whether people contribute and adopt knowledge (in the form of problems and solutions) in this distributive environment? This is to say, what affects knowledge sharing?
2. Organizational linkage question: Given that knowledge sharing does occur among the offices, what impact does this have on the office or the larger organization?

In the first question, we want to identify mechanisms that facilitate learning. In the second question, we want to identify the mechanisms that explain how learning and outcomes at one level affect activities, events, and outcomes at other levels. Both questions are very important. I am intrigued with why it is so difficult to share knowledge in this distributed environment. I am also curious, when this sharing occurs, whether sharing has effects. This chapter focuses on the second question, but our analysis should be relevant to general issues of organizational learning.

Organizational Linkages and Organizational Learning

To motivate the distinction between these questions, I present a brief foray into the organizational learning literature. There are many excel-

lent reviews (e.g., Huber, 1991; Miner & Mezias, 1996) about this literature. My intention is to be illustrative, not comprehensive. I want to
highlight some reasons for both disconnecting and connecting both
research questions.

There is a substantial body of theoretical work on organizational
learning (e.g., Argyris & Schon, 1978; Cyert & March, 1963; March,
1991; Miner & Mezias, 1996). Indeed, many observers of this literature
have pointed to the major focus on theory building rather than empirical research (Miner & Mezias, 1996). A cursory view of this literature
reveals the hard problems it has tried to tackle. Simply defining what
organizational learning means and distinctions between individual,
group, and organizational learning is a difficult task (Argote, 1999;
Argote & Epple, 1990; Huber, 1991; Weick & Westley, 1996). Another
difficult set of problems arises in understanding different learning processes, such as learning by doing and learning from others (Argote,
1999; Miner & Mezias, 1996), and different types of learning such as incremental versus radical (March, 1991; Miner & Mezias, 1996). All of
these excellent discussions delineate the meaning of organizational
learning, its processes, and its antecedents. Our current focus is complementary. In effect, we ask, given learning by doing or learning from
others, what are the consequences of these activities for other units or
levels of analysis?

The number of empirical papers regarding organizational learning
has increased rapidly in the last decade. What is striking is that this research appears at multiple levels of analysis—individual, group, organization, and population of organizations—using a variety of methods
from qualitative case studies (Adler & Cole, 1993), to econometric
modeling (Argote & Epple, 1990; Epple, Argote, & Devadas, 1991), to
simulations (Lant & Mezias, 1992). This work has been very thoughtful
and carefully done, grounding some of the theoretical work into real
organizational settings and/or good data sets and analytical models.

Moreland (1999) and his associates have done a series of experiments on the nature of transactive memory and work group performance. *Transactive memory* refers to the shared awareness members
have about who knows what in the work group. In our context, if training or other procedures strengthen a group's transactive memory and
performance, we want to know how these changes in activities and outcomes at the group level affect activities and outcomes at other units or
levels.

Argote (1999) and associates built an impressive program of research to understand learning curves in different organizational settings (e.g., shipyards, auto plants, pizza stores). The learning curves display the impacts of learning by doing or experience on the changes in an outcome variable, such as cost per unit of production. One focal question of this research has been to understand variations in these learning curves. Some of the investigated factors included forgetting, turnover of employees, learning from others, and whether knowledge is embedded in technology, the organization, or people.

Although I come back to this research in more detail later in the chapter, it is both similar and different from our focus in the following way. In their study of pizza stores, Darr, Argote, and Epple (1995) looked at the issue of knowledge sharing, an area I introduced in the beginning of the chapter. They show that certain organizational arrangements (i.e., being a member of a franchise) enhances learning and store-level outcomes. Our focus would build on that finding and ask how changes in knowledge sharing at the store level and costs per unit affected the larger organization. Also, they have studied truck plants, which operate in a lean manufacturing environment, similar to the plants we discussed in Chapter 6. Their research demonstrates that learning by doing and knowledge transfer between shifts affects plant-level outcomes. Our linkage analysis complements this research in two ways. First, it asks that if learning and positive outcomes occur within some units of the plant, how do these changes affect plant-level outcomes? In much of the learning-by-doing research, information is collected at the plant level but not at the individual, group, or unit levels. Therefore, cross-level effects are inferred but not studied (see a similar discussion of lean production systems in Chapter 6). The second question is, what are the impacts of plant-level changes on corporate-level changes (see the discussion of Champion International in Chapter 6)?

Although there are many excellent organizational learning research studies at other levels of analysis—the interorganizational level (Ingram & Baum, 1997) and population (Haunschild & Beckman, 1999)—I want to turn to three different cases of organizational learning at the firm level and examine how linkage analysis may add to our understanding and complement work on organizational learning. This examination continues the focus of this book on levels.

Case 8A: Learning in a
Distributed Environment

A distributed environment is a setting with a large number of units from the same organization that are performing the same functions. The units are geographically distributed and independent from each other. Because they are facing the same problems, there are obviously advantages to sharing knowledge with each other. For example, we did research in a large office equipment manufacturing firm, which had sales and service offices throughout the world. A class of equipment was experiencing downtime throughout the company, and one of the service groups discovered a solution. Providing this solution to other offices should contribute to both customer satisfaction and reduced costs. We observed in another study in a global consulting firm that one office designed an innovative process reengineering and system implementation for an aquarium, a unique organization. Other offices learned about this "new solution" and inquired about the processes. Again, by sharing this information, other offices were able to generate new revenue, opportunities, and solutions.

Despite these apparent advantages, there are many inhibitors to such an exchange. Formulating and communicating the process approach for the aquariums to other offices is time-consuming. The focus of attention within the offices is local, not corporate. Searching for solutions to the machine downtime problem is costly. Matching one office's definition of the problem and solution with another office in a different setting takes time (for a detailed description of inhibitors, see Goodman & Darr, 1998).

Even if we assume that exchanges do occur (the learning question), we cannot be sure whether they had any effects. In the study of the office equipment manufacturer (Goodman & Darr, 1996), we asked our respondents to describe the "most effective" best practice they had recently adopted. Of the 78 people we interviewed across four offices, 69 had adopted a best practice. Figure 8.1 displays what happened to these adopted practices. Some were not implemented. For those that were implemented, the effects on office-level indicators were known in some cases, but not in others. The impact of the most effective solutions was on specific technical solutions or on interim results. Only two directly affected office-level criteria (e.g., customer satisfaction, return on assets).

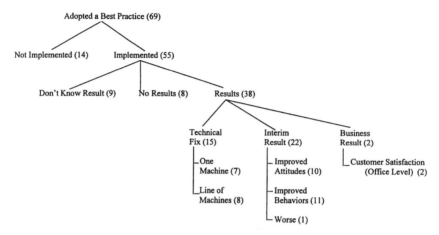

Figure 8.1. Consequences of Best Practice Exchange

In this company, even though it prided itself on knowledge sharing, you really do not see many bottom-line results at the office or corporation levels. At the same time, our interviews indicated there were a lot of best practice exchanges going on, both within and between offices.

What are some of the underlying features in this setting that will help us understand the relation between learning and outcomes at one level and the impact of these at other levels?

1. What is being exchanged? Much of what is being exchanged are small, incremental improvements, not fundamental changes in products or processes. If a service person solves a downtime problem, that is a clear benefit, but it is only one of the many transactions affecting the customer's satisfaction with the office equipment manufacturer. Therefore, the extent to which the exchange is fundamental in nature should help us determine whether learning and outcome changes at one level will lead to outcome changes in other units and levels. Stated in another way, exchanges that modify core versus peripheral activities should lead outcome changes at other levels. Later in this chapter, I give examples of some fundamental or core changes in product and processes design. These changes came about through exchanges in tacit knowledge (Nonaka & Takeuchi, 1995) and are likely to have significant impacts on multiple units and levels.

2. How widely adopted is the knowledge sharing? In the example about the aquarium, an important issue is how many people know about this innovation. If one person learns about this development, learning remains at the individual level, and the effect on the larger organization will not be observable. If the knowledge about the innovation is accessible in various organizational memory systems

(Olivera & Goodman, 1998), widely publicized, and adopted throughout the firm, then the learning activities and outcomes are likely to have effects at the organizational level.

3. A third factor may be the frequency of different types of exchanges, that is, our examples have been about a specific type of exchange (e.g., improving a particular machine's reliability or a process reengineering plan). We also need to look at the frequency of different types of exchanges. Putting these three factors together, we would expect that exchanges that are (a) fundamental, (b) widely adopted, and (c) frequent should change the probability that learning activities and outcomes at the individual level should affect office- and corporate-level outcomes.

Let's pursue this analysis by turning to an exotic example presented by Darr et al. (1995). The setting is pizza stores, and the incident is innovations for placing pepperoni on pan pizza. The problem was that in cooking pan pizzas, the pepperoni would migrate to the center. That was a poor-quality product. One solution was to monitor the pizza during baking and modify the placement of pepperoni. This was an expensive solution. Another solution developed at a store in western Pennsylvania was to place the pepperonis in the spokes around the pie, and, during cooking, the pepperoni becomes evenly distributed around the pie. Success! This innovation was copied by other stores in the same franchise. Later, at a meeting of all stores in the region, the innovation was discussed and broadly implemented. Company communications and the role of a consultant diffused the innovation to 90% of the stores.

This example captures distributed learning that led to a cost reduction and was widely adopted. Do these changes at the store level have implications for the firm? Let's return to some of our basic tools.

Outcome Coupling

The metrics between the stores (regional/organization or corporation) are likely to be the same—the number of pizzas sold, revenue, and costs. The form of organizing is additive, which means changes in store outcomes should directly affect corporate outcomes. The number of intermediary activities—boxing and delivery—is small. Also, the time delay between changes in costs or revenues should only be limited by the accounting system that records monthly outcomes. Therefore, there should be a fairly direct relation between store and corporate outcomes.

Limiting Conditions

In Chapter 5, we identified factors that might limit changes at one unit from affecting another. Given the relatively simple production process, it is unlikely that production capacity constraints or negative consequences for other units would be limiting factors. Also, the changes have been made in the core production process, which should have direct effects on costs.

An important concept in Chapter 5 was the idea of relative contributions. The question is, to what extent did this new production process improve costs and generate revenue? This is a harder question because you need to know how this particular product affected direct and indirect costs at the store level. In other words, we need to know whether this new process represents a fundamental change in costs for this product. Then, you need to estimate the effect of the new production process on total costs. If pan pizzas are a relatively low-demand product and they contribute in a minor way to costs, the impact of the production innovation at the store level is likely to be insignificant. In that scenario, even if 90% of the stores "learned the new process," we would not expect to see changes at the organizational level. On the other hand, if this and other new innovations significantly reduced costs at the store level, and 90% of the stores were using these innovations, then we might expect learning through knowledge sharing at the store level to increase outcomes at the corporate levels. In this scenario, when there are frequent, different exchanges, fundamental in nature, and the exchanges are widely diffused, there may be some positive feedback among these exchanges that tightens the connection between changes at the store and corporate level. This would parallel the "community of plants" concept that was presented in the Champion International case analysis in Chapter 6.

Case 8B: Learning in a
Lean Manufacturing Setting

I introduce a case regarding lean manufacturing because I want to present different environments for organizational learning and position the organizational linkage analysis in these different environments. This is one way to sharpen the similarities and dissimilarities between mechanisms that affect organizational learning and organizational linkage. I also selected this particular case because we already have discussed lean manufacturing systems from a linkage perspective (see Chapter 6). This should both shorten and sharpen this particular analysis.

There are several streams of learning research on learning and lean production systems. As part of their program on research on learning curves, Epple, Argote, and Murphy (1996) studied plant startups in truck plants in the auto industry. Their research demonstrated the basic learning curve effect, that is, direct labor hours per truck decreased at a decreasing rate as the cumulative number of trucks produced increased. When one of the plants moved from a one-shift to a two-shift operation, they were able to demonstrate that knowledge acquired during the one-shift operation carried forward to the period of the two-shift operation and was almost complete within 2 weeks of the second shift startup. One of the challenges during the shift-one start-up was learning how to reconfigure the technology and organizational procedures for producing trucks. The second shift had the advantage of using this knowledge that was embedded in the revised technological and organizational structure. The contribution in this kind of research is that they build detailed longitudinal data sets and can tease out this form of structural learning by examining natural experiments, such as the move from a one- to two-shift operation.

In another article on learning curves in manufacturing, Argote and Epple (1990) showed the learning curves for the three truck plants. Although they have the same general functional form, they also are different. What's interesting about the three learning curves is that the plants are all from the same company, producing the same new product, and all are in a start-up mode. At the same time, there are differences among the plants. Two are in the United States, but in different settings. The other plant is in Canada, works for a different division of the same company, and has a different union. One of the plants uses a form of team-based assembly. There also are differences in organizational dimensions such as the rigidity of job classifications. One interesting question is, if the plants are demonstrating learning but at different rates, what are some of the explanatory mechanisms? Would understanding changes in activities at the group and unit levels help us understand the differences in the learning curves? Here is where linkage analysis could inform learning research.

Another research approach to learning in lean production settings is presented by Adler and Cole (1993). Let's look at this case in more detail. They contrasted two auto plants—the Toyota-GM joint venture, NUMI, and Volvo's Uddevalla plant. Their first analysis suggested that the NUMI plant outperforms the Uddevalla plant in terms of productivity and quality. Also, they noted that the workers' quality of work life, although not ideal, is acceptable.

Their second analysis points to organizational learning as a key ingredient to the differences. They argued, "The Japanese production model explicitly focuses on strategies for organizational learning. Standardization of work methods is a pre-condition for achieving this end" (Adler & Cole, 1993, p. 92). Standardization captures best practices and facilitates diffusion of improvements throughout the organization. In the Uddevalla plant, where team autonomy and decentralization are central organizing principles, organizational learning and its diffusion are less likely (Adler & Cole, 1993).

Now, there is a rejoinder article by Berggren (1994), who argued that Adler and Cole's (1993) productivity comparisons are probably not correct. He also argued that the structure of the Volvo plant did lead to learning, particularly in areas such as very efficient model changeovers, an important factor in productivity and cost.

My interest is not to mediate this dispute. Rather, it is to draw a picture and show some of the intellectual gaps. The picture is of assembly plants (truck or auto). We know there has been a movement to lean production settings. We also know that focusing solely on the technological systems is incorrect. From MacDuffie's (1995; MacDuffie & Pil, 1997) work and our analysis in Chapter 6, the combination of technological and social arrangements seem to be critical to understanding effectiveness in lean manufacturing.

The basic argument in Chapter 6 and in this chapter is the same: If you want to learn about the effectiveness of lean production settings, whether you use metrics such as direct labor hours or defects per car, you need to understand how individual- or group-level activities and outcomes contribute to organizational outcomes and how changes in organizational-level structure and technology affect group and individual activities and outcomes. Let's assume that learning at the group level, as Adler and Cole (1993) suggested, explains productivity and quality differences at the plant level. I would like to take NUMI or

Uddevalla and trace learning activities and outcomes at the individual to group and group to organizational level. I would use the same strategy as developed in Chapter 6.

1. What are the basic features of outcome coupling in these plants—metrics, form of organizing, number of intermediary activities, programmed activities, time delay?
2. What are the limiting conditions in terms of constraints, negative consequences, or intervention in core or peripheral activities?
3. How does the organizational and technological environment shape the problem-solving, coordinating, focus-of-attention, and commitment processes?

The reader should refer back to Chapter 6 for a more detailed analysis of lean production systems. We argued that this is a complicated environment. Outcomes among units and the plant are not the same. The sequential form of organizing has many intermediary activities that follow a fixed sequence. There are likely to be many constraints and possible negative consequences. Therefore, asserting that learning at the individual or group level increases plant-level productivity is a big jump.

To bridge the individual and group-level learning on plant-level outcomes, we argued for some bridging or compensatory processes—multiple coordination mechanisms, focus of attention, and commitment, that is, improving learning and outcomes at one unit in a lean auto or truck plant may have no impact on plant-level outcomes. However, processes that elicit coordination across units; focus attention on individual-, unit-, and plant-level outcomes; and create commitment are more likely to generate correlated unit- and plant-level changes. The basic idea is that we can enhance the studies of organizational learning and of lean production settings by tracing how changes (learning or other processes) at one level have implications for other levels.

We also could look at the impact of the changes at the plant level to the division level, that is, let's assume that learning contributed to outcome improvement at the group, unit, and plant levels. Another target for linkage analysis is to trace whether plant-level changes in productivity, costs, or quality affected division-level indicators. The analysis of Champion International in Chapter 6 provides guidance for this type of linkage analysis.

Case 8C: Knowledge Creation—
New Products

The third case draws from the very interesting book by Nonaka and Takeuchi, *The Knowledge-Creating Company* (1995). I selected this case for several reasons. First, it is quite different from the prior two cases in terms of learning environments—the focus is on creating new products. Second, the role of tacit and explicit knowledge is fundamental in their book. In Case 8A and, to some extent, in Case 8B, the focus has been more on explicit knowledge. Their book also is multilevel focused. For example, there is an important concept called "cross-leveling," which deals with the movement of knowledge across different organizational entities.

It is quite difficult to summarize a book into part of a chapter. My strategy here is to capture some of their basic ideas and then draw on one of their examples to illustrate knowledge creation across levels of analysis. Then, I match some of the linkage ideas to the case. One central idea in Nonaka and Takeuchi's 1995 book is the role of tacit and explicit knowledge. Tacit knowledge is more subjective, context-specific, and hard to formalize and communicate. Explicit knowledge is more objective and can be formalized and communicated. Knowledge conversion is the interaction between the two forms of knowledge. This leads to four modes of knowledge conversion—tacit to tacit (as in an apprenticeship role), tacit to explicit (discovering tacit ideas and formalizing them), explicit to explicit (exchanging facts), and explicit to tacit (beliefs are internalized). This knowledge conversion process starts at the individual level and moves to "communities of interaction that cross sectional, departmental, divisional, and organizational boundaries" (Nonaka & Takeuchi, 1995, p. 72). The interactions among these four modes of knowledge conversion occur in five phases—sharing tacit knowledge, moving from tacit to explicit concepts, justifying concepts, building archetypes, and cross-leveling knowledge. There are also enablers that facilitate this process, such as autonomy and redundancy.

Let's move to the concrete case as a way of grounding their concepts and then making the transition to organizational linkage analysis. The setting is the recently merged Cooking Appliance Division of Matsushita, a large Japanese conglomerate. The market for household products was mature, price competition was severe, and profits were dropping. The

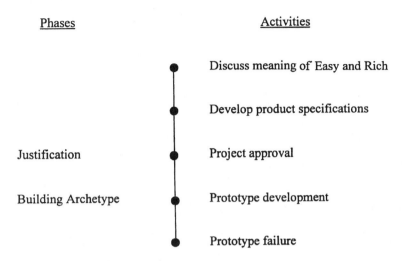

Phases

Activities

Discuss meaning of Easy and Rich

Develop product specifications

Justification

Project approval

Building Archetype

Prototype development

Prototype failure

Figure 8.2. Home Bakery—Cycle 1

intent of the merger was to improve operational efficiency. Only small operational benefits occurred.

At the time of this story, which is 1984, two events took place. First, a team came up with a new division concept called "Easy and Rich" to create delicious and nutritious food easily for the great number of working women. Second, the idea of an automatic home bakery machine was proposed by another firm. A connection between the Easy and Rich concept and the "Home Bakery" machine was made, and development work began.

Nonaka and Takeuchi (1995) then identified the following cycles of product development:

The project team meets to discuss the meaning of Easy and Rich and how it relates to the Home Bakery product. Eventually, product specifications are developed, and the product is submitted and approved by the company. A prototype was developed but produced a poor bread product (see Figure 8.2 for a description of activities and phases in the knowledge creation process).

To understand bread making, the next cycle begins as one of the team members went to work for a master baker. This was initially a tacit-tacit knowledge conversation between the master baker and team member. The team member, by making bread, was trying to learn some of the

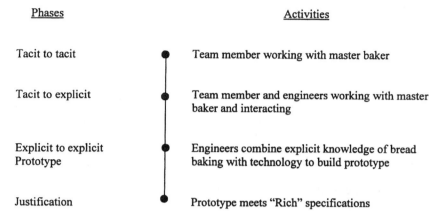

Figure 8.3. Home Bakery—Cycle 2

key processes from the master baker. Then, some of the engineering members of the team joined the bread-making apprenticeship. Over time, some of the tacit knowledge about bread making had been made explicit, particularly the kneading process. This was a fundamental change. Then, the engineers were able to construct a machine that represented some of the activities of the master bread maker (see Figure 8.3).

The third cycle focused on commercialization (see Figure 8.4). The project team was broadened to tie in manufacturing and marketing. The project moved from the lab to the division. The major challenge in commercialization was meeting certain cost targets, and there were many roadblocks. Eventually, the team developed some fundamental process changes, which substantially reduced costs. The product was placed in the market early in 1987 with great success. More than 500,000 units were sold in Year 1, far beyond expectations. In a short time, Home Bakery was selling worldwide, well beyond expectations (note that information about manufacturing and product launch is not discussed in Nonaka and Takeuchi's book).

The last cycle was cross-leveling of knowledge within and across divisions. The success of Home Bakery spread through the division. The manifestations in the division were twofold. First, the introduction of an automatic coffee brewer and rice cooker shortly followed, building off the Easy and Rich concept. Second, according to Nonaka and

Phases   Activities

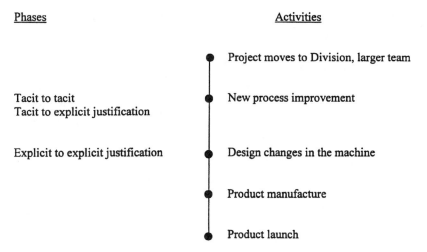

Project moves to Division, larger team

Tacit to tacit
Tacit to explicit justification   New process improvement

Explicit to explicit justification   Design changes in the machine

Product manufacture

Product launch

Figure 8.4. Home Bakery—Cycle 3

Takeuchi (1995, pp. 110-113), new knowledge and beliefs, some tacit and some explicit, were adopted throughout the division. These beliefs were that

- Innovative products can be developed through cooperation.
- Consumers respond to products that fulfilled Easy and Rich.
- Engineers develop products by interfacing with customers.
- Pursue quality without constraints.

If we examine this case from a learning perspective, one central question is: Why was the product development team so successful? Some of the explanations by Nonaka and Takeuchi (1995) include

- A clear meta goal—Easy and Rich
- Clear product specifications
- An autonomous team
- Commitment to a new product
- Diversity in group composition

In addition, a key event was the work with the master baker, which included tacit to tacit, tacit to explicit, and, eventually, explicit to explicit knowledge conversions. This led to a major breakthrough in product

design. Later, there were some other breakthroughs in reducing product costs. Again, the different knowledge conversion processes were
critical.

If we examine the case from the linkage perspective, one central
question is, how did the activities and outcomes of the product development team lead to changes in activities and outcomes at the division
level? First, there was the successful launch of the Home Bakery product. Second, there was the successful development and launch of other
similar products. Let's consider the relation between the product development team and the successful launch at the organizational level.

Outcome Coupling

The outcome metrics of the product development team are different
from the metrics of the Cooking Appliance Division. The form of organizing is sequential from development to commercialization to manufacturing to distribution. There are many intermediary activities within
each of these major sequences. The time period between product development approval to initial sales was more than 2 years. All these features reduce the potential impact of outcomes from the product development team on division outcomes.

Limiting Conditions

In terms of limiting conditions, factors such as constraints and negative consequences are more likely in a complicated sequential arrangement than in an additive arrangement such as the pizza stores. Unfortunately, the authors do not explore the sequence of activities after the
product is handed to manufacturing, so we do not know much about
constraints and negative consequences. However, these limiting conditions are likely to be evident. On the other hand, the development of a
new product is clearly a core activity. In terms of relative contribution,
information is provided on sales, but we do not have information on
the relative contribution of Home Bakery to the economic performance of the Cooking Appliance Division. We do know, however, that
sales of the other products and profitability were in decline and Home
Bakery sales were higher than expectations.

This initial analysis suggests a mixed picture of whether new activities and outcomes of the product development level will affect division-level outcomes.

Process Mechanisms

The process mechanisms presented in Chapter 6 may provide some additional insight into why Home Bakery was a success:

- There were some very good team problem-solving processes, both in the product development team and later in the commercialization team. The problem-solving processes revolved around knowledge conversion processes between tacit and explicit knowledge. There were fundamental or core breakthroughs in product design, which contributed to new product features and to meeting cost goals. Without these changes, there would have been no product. The key word is "fundamental" versus "incremental" problem solving.

- There was a common focus of attention, both in terms of the metagoals and product specifications, that were shared by multiple actors, both tacitly and explicitly over time. When the commercial team was created, it included members of the original team plus others (e.g., marketing) who would have downstream responsibilities. This permitted tacit to tacit, tacit to explicit, and explicit to explicit knowledge conversion between new and old members. Developing these shared understandings or common focus probably facilitated the successes in the commercialization team and downstream activities.

- Coordination was achieved by a common focus of attention, centering around the Easy and Rich concept and adherence to product specifications, which reflected production and marketing considerations. The development of these tacit understandings represents a form of coordination. There were probably many other coordination mechanisms after the product "hand-off," but these were not discussed in the book.

- Commitment and motivation levels seemed high, at least up to the period of production. Successfully solving major problems and developing shared goals all contributed to enhancing levels of commitment and motivation. Probably removing the major design and cost obstacles reinforced the level of motivation, not only for the team members but also for those along the value chain such as manufacturing and sales.

Despite some of the inhibitors discussed under outcome coupling and limiting conditions, these processes probably account for the success of the product and its spillover in creating new products and a different product development culture.

I want to note that the Home Bakery product team had broader impacts beyond the successful launch of that product. A year later, there was a successful launch of an automatic coffee maker, to be followed by a rice cooker the following year. The reader will immediately recognize that these products are also designed to make cooking easier, there is a strong emphasis on high quality ("rich"), and there is a common technological infrastructure that makes all three of the products work.

If we were to extend the earlier linkage analysis that focused on the product development team → commercialization team → manufacturing → marketing and sales, there would be other horizontal and vertical linkages. One analysis would focus on the relation between the Home Bakery team and other product developments. What were some of the mechanisms (e.g., personnel movement, formal publicity, and informal stories) by which some of the tacit and explicit concepts such as Easy and Rich, interacting with customers, changed the activities and outcomes of other product development teams? Another analysis might focus on the team- and division-level personnel. The initial success of both the product and commercialization teams (e.g., product design breakthroughs, cost savings) should have been very visible to senior division managers prior to the successful product launch. Again, the outcomes of these teams should have influenced the beliefs and practices of senior management and staff about the Easy and Rich concept. By articulating these concepts and others about being close to the customer and innovative products, it is likely the other product development teams were supported by senior management, and a broader shared understanding of these ideas permeated the divisions. These changes serve to focus people's attention and to coordinate and elicit commitment around this cultural change. Unfortunately, Nonaka and Takeuchi (1995) do not provide more details so that we could trace some of these linkages.

Concluding Thoughts

- The analyses of organizational learning and organizational linkages are independent and complementary.
- The former focuses on why learning occurs in the distributed environments of the pizza stores or in the product development team of the Home Appliance Division.

- The organizational linkage analysis takes the learning activities and outcomes at a particular level as given and then explores the impact of this learning on other units or levels of analysis.
- In the three learning cases, I have examined the impacts of learning on other levels by looking at
  — Outcome coupling
  — Limiting conditions
  — The process mechanisms
  — The feedback mechanisms

In each of these cases, these linkage analysis tools helped us to understand whether learning and outcomes observed at one level would or would not affect outcomes in another unit or level. Outcome coupling provides an initial mapping of relations across units or levels and whether the impacts are likely to be direct. In the pizza store example, outcomes were the same across levels and impacts were likely to be direct. The limiting conditions specify inhibitors to changes across levels and units. In the lean auto manufacturing environments, there are likely to be many inhibitors. That is why I would like to see more attention in research similar to that of Adler and Cole (1993) to be more explicit about how group learning and outcome changes affect unit- and plant-level changes. Tracing these linkages should be explicit in organizational research. The process mechanisms, coupled with feedback mechanisms, provide an explanation of how changes do occur across levels in complicated environments. The Home Bakery case is an important illustration of this point.

Conversation Eight

You: Most of your examples have focused on operating units such as a plant or the relation between a plant and the larger corporation. Yet, there is growing research on interorganizational learning and learning at the population level.

PSG: I think the basic ideas in this chapter can be expanded to other units of analysis. If you think back, we have examined the linkages among individual, group, unit, organizational unit (e.g., a plant or store), and the corporate level of analysis. If we looked at other organizational forms such as learning between a hotel and chain (Ingram & Baum, 1997), I think the tools of linkage analysis would be equally applicable. For example, let's say the advantage of chain affiliation is in the acquisition of infrastructure such as a reservation or accounting system. A linkage analysis would trace how these changes affected the hotel's performance. Also, we could look at how the hotel's performance affected chain performance.

You: I'm not convinced about the distinction between learning and linkages.

PSG: Well, let's go back to the first example about the office equipment manufacturer. This organization has multiple units around the world performing the same function. Let's assume that, either through introducing new technology and/or creating a culture for learning, we can document exchanges across units. This is an example of learning. The linkage analysis focuses on whether the learning led to outcome changes at the unit and at the organizational level. Do increases in knowledge sharing at the worker level improve unit and organizational performance?

In many ways, I see the learning and linkage approaches as very complementary. In many ways, linkage analysis is about making explicit untested assumptions. If you think that knowledge sharing among offices or units is beneficial, let's make explicit how these exchanges lead to beneficial outcomes at different units or levels of analysis. Although this connection is often asserted, there are few empirical studies of knowledge sharing in distributed environments that link learning processes and organizational effectiveness indicators. If you think certain organizational forms facilitate learning and outcomes at the plant level, show us how it works. The essence of the Adler-Cole argument is that learning leads to organizational effectiveness. This and related studies do measure learning and effectiveness indicators, but they do not conceptually or empirically explain how or why this relation unfolds. What are the mechanisms by which learning and performance changes at the individual or group levels affect plant-level outcomes? Linkage analysis opens up the "black box" and makes causal processes more explicit.

9 Reflecting Backward
and Looking Forward

In Chapter 1, I introduced our two basic tasks: to delineate the concept of organizational linkages and to present and illustrate some tools for linkage analysis. The principal focus was on tracing changes of activities and outcomes in one unit or level on changes in activities and outcomes at another unit or level. What are the conditions in which we would expect no "cross-level" effects, and when might these effects be amplified across levels or units?

Let's think back to the productivity paradox, which was posed as an interesting application area. The productivity paradox says there is little relation between investments in information technology and intended productivity improvements. For example, suppose a firm introduces information technology (computers) to improve the productivity of its customer service representatives. And suppose that the number of calls processed per hour increased due to the new information technology, but these positive gains had no impact on other units or levels of the organization. Linkage analysis begins with two important facets of this problem. First, the investment was successful in terms of improving productivity at the customer service level. (If it were not successful, the research problem would be more about ineffective implementation than organizational linkage analysis.) Second, there was an assumption that changes at the customer service level would go beyond the unit and contribute to corporate level changes. Studying organizational problems of this nature requires the tools of organizational linkage analysis.

Tools for Linkage Analysis

To aid in this analysis, a set of tools has been developed (see Figure 9.1). Although different combinations of these tools can be used for different problems, there seems to be a general sequence in applying the tools.

1. Build an initial chart of the social system. Define the critical actors, both internally and externally, to the system (see Figures 3.4 and 3.5), and identify the time period for analysis. This chart will surely change as your analysis evolves, but you need a chart at the starting point.

2. Examine and describe each element of the outcome coupling concepts (Figure 3.2):
   —Are the metrics the same across levels?
   —Are the outcomes embedded in additive, sequential, or reciprocal forms of organizing?
   —What is the number of intermediary activities? Are they programmed? What are the time delays between changes in outcomes at one level and their impact on other levels?

   Outcome coupling provides the first order of explanation in linkage analysis. To the extent that (a) the metrics are different, (b) forms of organizing are sequential or reciprocal, (c) the number of activities are large and programmed, and (d) the time delays are long, we would expect little or no impacts of successful changes within the unit (customer service department) on other units or levels in this organization.

3. Observe the limiting conditions discussed in Chapter 5, including constraints to the social system, negative consequences, and where changes occur. Holding constant the forms of outcome coupling (e.g., similar outcome metrics, large number of intermediary activities), the existence of constraints, negative consequences, and whether the changes in activities and outcomes occur in core or peripheral areas will determine whether improvements at one unit will affect others.

   In Chapter 5, I cited an example in which the intervention in information technology increased the productivity of customer service representatives but reduced the productivity of their supervisor. These contrary effects explain why positive changes for one group of workers might not affect other units or levels. Increases in the number of constraints, negative consequences, and interventions in peripheral areas reduce the likelihood of changes in one area affecting another.

   Another concept introduced in Chapter 5 is the relative contribution of outcomes at one level or unit on another. The production function sharpens our thinking about the relative contribution of one unit to the large organizational entity. In the Champion International case, a key question was the relative contribution of a particular plant to the productivity of the corporation. In the pizza case, there was learning across 90% of the stores in terms of reducing the costs for

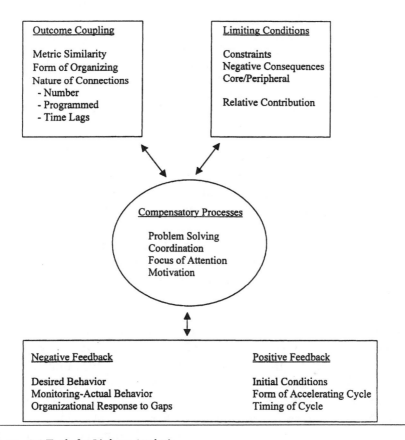

Figure 9.1 Tools for Linkage Analysis

a particular product. However, a key question was the relative contribution of that production change to total revenue and costs of the store and corporation. Assessing empirically or conceptually *ex ante,* the relative contribution of a particular unit or product to changes in the firm's production function is an important step in estimating changes of one unit on another.

4. Examine the processes, such as problem solving, multiple coordination, and focus of attention, which can be thought of as compensatory or countervailing forces. If we map out a setting in which outcomes or metrics are different, the form of organizing is sequential, and the number of intermediary activities is great, the probability is low that changes in one level or unit will affect others. However, if, as I described in the lean manufacturing case (Chapter 6), there are powerful problem-solving and coordinating mechanisms, these processes can offset the limiting conditions and facilitate changes at one level to affect another.

5. Analyze the underlying feedback mechanisms. If there is synergy among these processes, the probability of cross-level effects is increased. In Chapter 6, I diagrammed (Figure 6.2) how problem-solving and continuous-improvement processes can interact in a positive feedback cycle. This, in turn, can enhance other processes such as coordination, focus of attention, and commitment, which, in turn, can enhance the problem-solving and continuous-improvement processes. This interacting cycle of processes can offset some of the limiting conditions and perhaps amplify the impact of one level on another.

An interesting issue is whether the basic classes of tools (outcome coupling, limiting conditions, processes, and feedback mechanisms) are too unwieldy or too many for any linkage analysis. I believe not. The phenomena I am examining are very complex. The Barings case is about a complicated set of organizational arrangements. Also, I am interested in dynamic, not static, systems. Understanding change activities over time, as illustrated in Champion International (Chapter 6) or Analog Devices (Chapter 7), requires the application of all four classes of tools.

A related question is whether these tools are equally applicable across a range of organizational domains or problem areas. I think the tools are generalizable. The problem areas of errors, change, and learning are different, yet the application of the tools seems important and relevant. We considered outcome coupling (e.g., similarity of metrics and forms of organizing) across all three domains. The concept of relative contribution seems pertinent whether we are examining the impact of process changes in pizza stores and their impact on the corporation, or whether we are examining the potential losses incurred at the Barings Singapore office to the potential losses at Barings. The positive and negative feedback cycles are relevant for understanding the demise of Barings or the success at Champion International.

Organizational Linkage Analysis— A Distinctive Perspective

Throughout this book, I have argued that an organizational linkage represents a unique value-added concept. I have acknowledged ties to the levels literature (Roberts et al., 1978), the meso perspective (Rousseau & House, 1994), multilevel approaches to group performance (Hollenbeck et al., 1998), and multilevel human resources (HR) approaches to organizational performance (Lawler et al., 1998). The distinctiveness of the organizational linkage concept is that it (a) surfaces some basic organizational assumptions, that is, it moves implicit assumptions into an explicit arena; and (b) it provides some new lenses to generate previously unidentified research issues. Let's consider these two forms of distinctiveness.

Implicit Assumptions

Throughout this book, I have tried to point out persistent level biases or assumptions. For example, much of the literature on groups in organizations assumes that improving group performance will improve organizational performance. Much of the research beginning in the late 1970s to the present on self-managing teams (e.g., Goodman, Devadas, & Griffith Hughson, 1988) assumes that self-managing teams will be effective and this team level of effectiveness will be correlated with improvements in organizational effectiveness. This latter assumption (the correlation between team and organizational effectiveness) is an assumption that is both implicit and untested. Indeed, simply remembering my analysis of the dimensions of outcome coupling (Figure 3.2) or the discussion of limiting conditions (Chapter 5) would raise serious doubts that there may be any relation between self-managing team effectiveness and organizational effectiveness.

Similar implicit assumptions appear in my analyses of organizational change and learning. In the analysis of lean manufacturing facilities, I identified a set of technological and organizational features that were associated with high productivity in automobile assembly plants. Implicit in this specific array of technological and organizational features was the assumption that highly motivated and high-performance individuals and groups contributed to higher unit level productivity, which, in turn, was related to higher plant level productivity. Another assumption was that firms that did not have these technological and organizational features would not have the correlation between individual-, group-, unit-, and plant-level outcomes. What I pointed out in both examples of lean production systems in Chapter 6 (auto plants and paper plants) is that these are only assumptions. There has been no attempt to measure systematically and/or trace out effects across levels.

These could be individual or unit changes to plant outcomes or plant-level outcome changes in unit-, group-, or individual-level outcomes.

This same argument applies to the learning chapter (Chapter 8). In the comparison between the Toyota-GM joint venture (NUMI) and Volvo's Uddevalla plant, implicit assumptions are made that differences in learning and productivity improvement at one level will lead to plant-level differences. Unfortunately, there are not quantitative or qualitative data connecting group-level to plant-level outcomes. Also, there is no theoretical recognition of the difficulties and limiting conditions that would prevent group-level outcomes from affecting plant level outcomes. Remember, in this sequential form of organizing with many intermediary activities and limiting conditions, the correlation between group-, unit-, and plant-level outcomes is likely to be attenuated.

The distinctive feature of linkage analysis in making these implicit assumptions explicit is critical for theory development. If there is a theory about self-managing team effectiveness, it needs to be extended to account for conditions in which improvements in team effectiveness will lead to improvements in organizational effectiveness. Most theories about groups in organizations do not make the linkages explicit. Similarly, if one proposes a theory of multiple system change, which includes modifications in job design, reward systems, participation mechanisms, information policies, and HR policies (see Table 6.3), it should be incumbent on the theoretician to be explicit about how the theory works. One should say more than simply that there is an alignment of interests among workers, managers, union, and the company, or that there needs to be congruency among social and technical systems. This array of system changes should affect motivations and performance of individuals, groups, and units. How do these changes facilitate changes at one level from affecting another? Where are the limiting conditions I discussed in Chapter 5? Are there some offsetting forces, such as multiple coordination or focus-of-attention mechanisms, minimizing the effects of the limiting conditions? Unless we can move from this very general theorizing to more explicit attention to these critical linkages, our level of theory in terms of explanatory and predictive power will remain weak and primarily *ex post*. Becoming more explicit about linkages will sharpen our theoretical understanding of organizational processes and change.

New Research Issues

A second distinctive feature of linkage analysis is that it provides new lenses to think about different research questions. Let's review the three major application areas of this book and illustrate how linkage analysis identifies some new questions or surfaces.

Errors

One question in organizational errors research is the interaction among different types of errors over time. I distinguish between organizational errors, measurement errors, and design errors. Also, I distinguish between actual errors and latent errors. The analysis of both Barings and ValuJet showed how these errors feed off each other. In the Barings case, interaction among errors fueled the positive feedback cycle that was moving this system to be "out of control." We know very little about different forms of errors and how they interact and lead to negative organizational consequences. A related problem is that we know very little about the initiation and rates of change of positive feedback cycles in error research. It is clear that Perrow (1984) talked about interaction among failures in highly interactive, tightly coupled technical systems, which leads to accidents. But Barings is really about the interaction among errors that have human and organizational origins. There is no dominant technology. There is a complicated set of activities and outcomes that occur at different levels and over different time periods (see Figure 4.2). An important research question is whether, *ex ante,* we can identify the factors that initiate and accelerate this feedback cycle and how this cycle links individual activities and organizational outcomes. Another interesting problem is to better understand the role of context in organizational error research. I clearly selected two cases that greatly differed from the modal studies on organizational errors. In much of the research on errors, there are complicated technical systems such as nuclear power plants and aircraft carriers. Both Barings and ValuJet were largely about errors in human or social systems, but the contrast between the cases was extraordinary. The ValuJet case has a loosely coupled system with low interactive complexity. In both systems, there were design, measurement, and organizational errors, but in Barings, the system gradually accelerated out of control. Negative feedback systems were in place, but they did not work. In ValuJet, there were no negative feedback systems because there were no measurement systems in place. There were no accelerating positive feedback systems, yet 110 people died. Understanding different contextual impacts on how individual-level errors lead to organizational-level errors is an explicit challenge raised by the contrast between ValuJet and Barings.

Organizational Change

In my prior discussions about organizational change (Chapters 5-7), I pointed out that understanding the linkages among individual-, group-, unit-, and organizational-level outcomes is essentially unexplored. To make sense of these cross-level linkages requires good theoretical work. The organizational change improvement paradox is another problem derived from my analysis of the interaction of outcomes over time. In Chapter 7, we saw that a change effort led to positive changes in quality and costs over time, which later were associated with declining profit margins. Understanding how positive outcomes of change can eventually lead to negative organizational results is an interesting problem. This type of paradox would not be on the "radar screen" for most organizational researchers. This paradox requires tracking multiple outcomes of a change program over time. This type of research is not typically done.

In my analysis of the organizational change improvement paradox, I noted two other dilemmas. One is the diminishing return dilemma. Basically successful change efforts, over time, will bring the system to a point where it is difficult to extract any more gains that, in turn, will hurt the change effort, that is, change efforts initially focus on areas where there are easy wins. Over time, it is hard to extract more gains from these areas, and other areas are inherently more difficult. At this point, many of the positive feedback cycles that are driving the change across levels will slow down, and the delay between work and outcomes will increase, to the detriment of the change.

The work context dilemma, discussed in Chapter 7, is that rates of changes vary by work context (e.g., manufacturing vs. product development), but the rates of changes across work areas are not well understood. Therefore, work areas attracting the most success will attract more resources, although this allocation strategy may not be optimal for long-range change. I noted that in the Analog Devices case the failure to develop new products offset the benefits of improved quality and costs. The research challenge is to understand the nature of the organizational change improvement paradox and the diminishing returns dilemma and the work context dilemma, which contribute to the paradox. Understanding the conditions that facilitate or inhibit the diminishing returns or work context dilemmas are good starting points. Understanding *ex ante* when and where the improvement paradox is more likely to occur is a hard but exciting problem.

The linkage analysis of the plant-corporation relationship in the Champion International case raised another interesting research area. My analysis examined the impact of plant-level changes on corporate-level outcomes. The question I raised was whether the plant-level changes had an additive or synergistic effect on corporate-level outcomes such as productivity. The concept of "community of plants" suggests that although the changes at the plant level were initiated and designed individually, the knowledge of and interaction with the other plants created a shared understanding about the change. This shared understanding accelerated the change process at each plant. To some extent, this community of plants idea is similar to the "communities of practice" idea suggested by Brown and Duguid (1991). My focus is on knowledge sharing and motivation stimulated by other plants going through a similar process. Their focus is on informal knowledge sharing among employees in similar jobs. The research task is to identify and to understand the impact of these communities on organizational outcomes.

Organizational Learning

My linkage exploration into the learning area framed another group of research problems. Probably the most obvious challenge is to understand the effectiveness of learning on unit- or organizational-level outcomes. In the case of learning in distributed environments, in which knowledge in one part of the organization is shared with other parts, we do not know much about the impact of specific forms of sharing and changes in unit or organizational outcomes. Some of the factors—the frequency of sharing, the extent to which it was available to others, and the potential impact of what was shared—are predictors of the effectiveness of knowledge sharing. There are few, if any, studies that track this form of knowledge exchange on unit or organizational effectiveness.

Another research venture comes from my review on knowledge creation relative to new products. Nonaka and Takeuchi (1995) discussed knowledge conversion between tacit and explicit knowledge and within tacit and explicit knowledge. In my analysis of creation of a new product, there were some critical knowledge conversion points (e.g., from tacit knowledge of the master baker to explicit technical rules about twisting the dough). Understanding more about different forms of knowledge conversion seems particularly important. There is a major emphasis in the current learning literature on explicit to explicit knowledge conversions, but it omits tacit to explicit, implicit to implicit, or explicit to implicit exchanges. If we can identify the different forms of knowledge conversion, we may do a better job in understanding learning activities and their impact on the outcomes of other units and levels.

Organizational Mysteries

Organizational linkage analysis challenges some of the most common assumptions about organizational levels and the interrelations among outcomes across levels and units. The task is to move from implicit to explicit assumptions, reframe old problems, and map out the consequences of the change. Another distinctive feature of linkage analysis is the generation of new research opportunities that were discussed previously. This section focuses more on mysteries, things we do not or cannot know. As I worked through the content areas of errors, change, and learning in writing this book, I was struck as much by the mysteries as I was by how linkage analysis could help better understand organizational phenomena. I want to acknowledge some of these mysteries briefly. They are not original. They permeate our lives. They are part of completing a story.

Triggers

Throughout this analysis, unexpected external or internal events created the energy in our stories. In the Barings case, an earthquake affected the economy in Japan, and prices on the stock exchange dropped. The drop in prices, coupled with the overextended position of Barings, led to financial disaster. Now, instead of an earthquake, some other event (e.g., birth of a new industry, discovery of natural resources) might have driven the market up, and the trader would have been a hero rather than someone going to jail. In the ValuJet case, there was a series of triggers, some internal, some external. The movement of the canisters from the maintenance area to SabreTech shipping was not part of any standard operating procedure. They sat in maintenance for some time before someone decided to move them. The anticipated visit of a potential customer for SabreTech motivated a manager to clean up the area and send the canisters to ValuJet. Without these triggers, the canisters might not have made their way to Flight 592 or any other ValuJet plane. Also, further delay might have permitted identification of the canisters as hazardous. In the case of Champion International, the presence of the CEO during the change activities was both important for its sustainability and also a little unusual. There are many external and internal events that make the job tenure of most CEOs rather short. If that had happened at Champion International, perhaps the change effort would not have been sustainable, and we would not have learned about this change and related outcomes.

The idea of random triggers as uncontrollable events that have important organizational consequences is not new. However, these triggers played an important role in our stories, particularly how they ended. The acknowledgment of these unpredictable events does not diminish the importance of the linkage analysis. Barings was a system out of control. If it were not the earthquake and drop in stock prices, it probably would have been something else that would have led to its financial failure. In the ValuJet case, on the other hand, it is not so obvious that a plane crash would have occurred. The canisters might not have been sent, or they might have been placed in a cargo area where they might not have ignited. We will not know if another series of triggers would have led to 110 people dying.

Time

Issues about time permeate our linkage analysis. Some uses of time were fairly straightforward. In discussing the features of outcome coupling, we wanted to examine the time connection between outcomes at different levels. In the Barings case, a daily loss incurred by a trader would be immediately connected to losses at Barings Singapore and the parent company. In other contexts (e.g., group learning in a manufacturing plant), there would be longer delays between outcomes.

In other cases, the role of time is more mysterious and less tractable. Positive feedback cycles are an important tool in linkage analysis. I used them in analysis of errors, change, and learning. Although the concept is clear, the form and timing of the cycles are not well understood. In analysis of the TQM change effort, I noted that the acceleration rates in a manufacturing setting and a product development setting were different. But I do not know how and when they will be different in any fine-grained predicted way. Knowing that the acceleration rates will begin slower in a product development setting is not that informative. There is a complex set of variables that interact with each other to launch the positive feedback cycle and probably a different set that signal a decline in the rates of these cycles. Little is known about the timing of these cycles. In our analysis of the product development process, I noted some important breakthroughs such as translating implicit practices of the baker into explicit technological processes. But that breakthrough was not the result of a slow, cumulative set of experiments. It came about because someone thought it was a good idea to apprentice with the baker. But it was not clear, *ex ante,* that one could identify critical practices of the baker or when this would happen. Even when the breakthrough occurred, it was not a necessary and sufficient condition for success. It was the breakthrough interacting with other variables plus later breakthroughs that accounted for a successful product. However, the time period for this process seems indeterminable. It is a product of some random as well interaction among some complex variables.

Analyzing *Ex Post* Versus *Ex Ante*

The data for linkage analysis come from stories or retrospective accounts. That should not detract from the analysis, because I wanted to embed the tools in real organizational events. However, it does point to a limiting condition—the fragility of stories or actual events.

The Analog Devices case in Chapter 7 looks at a change effort in terms of multiple outcomes over time. The organizational change improvement paradox was an important point in discussing how changes at individual and unit levels led to positive outcomes for the firm, but over time, these benefits led to unanticipated negative outcomes for the organization. However, why did the events at Analog Devices unfold as they did? There were many possible paths. Management might have maintained or increased their resource allocation into product development, and new products might have been generated. Given the increased capacity created by the TQM change activities, new products would have generated new profits or revenues. As I pointed out previously, breakthroughs in product development are not necessarily tied to some cumulative allocation in resources. If new products had been generated simply through a lucky convergence of circumstances, the problem with profit margins might have been offset. Or exogenous events might have slowed their competitors' use of TQM practices or enhanced their own market position.

The problem is, the linkage analysis has been implemented on *ex post* events. Someone has presented a story defined by time, social space, actors, and events. They have decided what is included and what is omitted. In Analog Devices, I do not have all the information to understand why new products were not created. We do not know why people were not more aware of the limitations on pricing policy. In ValuJet, we do not know why the safety caps were not available. In Champion International, we do not know why some plants were not productive.

The challenge for the researcher is using linkage analysis *ex ante*. In Chapters 3 to 8, I provided some very specific predictions based on the nature of the outcome coupling dimensions, the presence of limiting conditions, the compensatory processes, or the feedback mechanisms. We can identify conditions in which changes in activities and outcomes at one level or unit will or will not affect other levels or units. The challenge is applying these tools to a system that is affected by random triggers, a time structure that is difficult to specify, and a complex system of interacting events, with many unanticipated events. These pose a trip in very uncharted waters. The tools for linkage analysis will provide *ex ante* propositions, but the trip will be uneasy and can take many turns.

New Organizational Contexts

This book has focused largely on traditional forms of organizations. Mines, manufacturing plants, banks, and airlines all fall in this category. They have goals, structures, and processes. In general, people come to work with others at a particular time and setting. Our linkage analysis has been done in the broad context of these traditional organizations. Clearly, these organizations differ in many respects, such as the form of technology, the nature of the interdependence across operations, complexity, global perspective, and so on. But there are some broad commonalities in how they do their work.

Changes in technology, global economies, and demographics have facilitated the emergence of different forms of organizations. These new forms will both complicate linkage analysis and require some form of linkage analysis. For example, there is a new form of work teams, called exocentric (Goodman & Wilson, 1998), which primarily focuses on external activities. They differ from traditional teams in which people come to work in the same place and at the same time to internally coordinate a set of activities. Computer emergency response teams are one type of exocentric team. Their job is to prevent attacks on the Internet. They have a number of distinguishing features from traditional work teams. First, it is very hard to assess the effectiveness of what they do. Second, they meet as a team when an attack on the Internet is observed. This is infrequent and unpredictable. Third, teams reconfigure as to composition each time incidents arise, that is, each incident has a new team. Fourth, most of the individual's time is spent in interacting with people outside the organization. Other forms of exocentric teams are distributed in space and time (e.g., software production working on a 24-hour clock).

The difficulty of doing linkage analysis on these teams should be apparent. Unlike traditional organizations, there are no clear outcomes (such as tons of coal/hour). The teams are continually reconfiguring. A team might come together once or twice to send out an advisory about an attack and then disband. A new team will work on the next attack. Given this reconfiguration of teams and no visible outcomes, it is difficult to do a linkage analysis as I described previously in the coal mining team or self-designing team in manufacturing.

However, the linkage question is still relevant. These teams sit in a computer security unit that performs other functions, which, in turn, is in a large organization whose goal is to improve software effectiveness throughout the United States. The teams also are part of a network of similar computer security organizations around the world. Exploring how improvements in team performance contribute to unit, organizational, and network performance, as well as vice versa, seems to be a relevant question. The challenge is that doing the linkage analysis in this or in similar new forms of organizations will be different and much more difficult, although still relevant and important.

Methodological Approaches

It would be very difficult to read this book without asking, "How would you do an empirical study of organizational linkages?" Also, if you took the previous section on "organizational mysteries" seriously, can linkages be studied systematically? My view is that you can study organizational linkages. I have not chosen to emphasize methods or write a "methods" chapter because (a) the book is primarily about reframing in linkage terms how we think theoretically about certain organizational phenomena and (b) different methodological approaches permeate the book. Also, I do not think there are as yet 5 or 10 good models of linkage studies that I could use as reference points.

How could you get started in studying linkages? The first and most traditional step is to revert to the literature set out in Chapter 1 (see the section titled "Points of Convergence and Divergence—Existing Literatures"). Specifically, I am referring to new work on levels (Chan, 1998; Klein et al., 1994), new developments in meso research (Rousseau & House, 1994), and new developments in multilevel theory of group (Hollenbeck et al., 1998) and organizational phenomena (Lawler et al., 1998). This would provide an important base. Or you could go to some of the sources from this book. You have choices ranging from understanding the case studies in more detail (e.g., Champion International) to seeing a "system dynamics" approach (Sterman, 1994) used to map and analyze complex phenomena.

Another approach, which is more of a "thought experiment," is to rethink how you might redesign some of the studies cited in this book. Let's consider a few examples:

Barings

This is a classic case of sampling on the dependent variable, something one wants to avoid. But let's think of a new design prior to the emergence of a disaster such as bankruptcy. Banks are very sensitive to risks. They keep records on all kinds of risks, ranging from operational, market, trading, and so on. That means a longitudinal study could be designed that tracks measurement, design, and organizational errors in an actual (i.e., real negative consequences) or latent form. To begin with, these data could be arranged by the trader, by the unit to which the trader belongs, and by the larger organizational unit. You could track individual errors, how they interact with other errors, and, over time, look for impacts on the organization or unit.

Lean Production Systems

The problem in this research is that data are collected at the structural level (e.g., social and technical) and at the plant performance level. If we were to redesign this study, we want to get performance data at the individual, group, unit (e.g., body shop), and plant levels. If the structural changes and multilevel performance data were available over time, we could begin to understand how group unit-level changes might affect plant-level changes and vice versa.

Learning Curve Studies

These studies show how the unit cost of a product, measured at the plant level, decreases over time with experience. To better understand the shape of the learning curve or to account for differences across plants in learning curves, it would be useful to obtain information about cost structures at the group, unit, or staff levels. Also, it would be useful to trace the curves beyond the startup or initial equilibrium level and to examine why similar production organizations have different learning curves.

These thought experiments provide a beginning. They do not deal with the complex set of processes we have identified in these cases. But simply redoing the designs would provide some basic information for understanding what happens when traders exceed their trading limits, or how problem-solving innovations in a lean production system affect the flow.

A third approach to "doing" a linkage study examines "potential exemplars." These are empirical options to capture the detail, dynamic properties, and mysteries that characterize a linkage analysis. Here are some models.

Diane Vaughan's (1996) book on the Challenger is a case in point. This book has a number of important features. It has an extremely detailed, rich data set. The researcher's bias seems more in selecting information in rather than selecting information out. It has important historical data. The experiences in interpreting the state of the O-rings and their "fix" at each of the launches are critical. The book explores the roles of many actors directly and indirectly involved with the O-rings. Many paths are explored. Some go nowhere. Some represent good hypotheses, but they are disconfirmed. Some are confirmed. Anomalies and contradictions (forms of mysteries) are acknowledged. She built a large, longitudinal, multiple-constituency database. It is not just the data. She was a detective at work looking at data, following up on leads, and looking for confirming or disconfirming information. This is truly hard work! Writing a case is different.

Another exemplar of this third approach is work of the system dynamics researchers. The analysis in Chapter 7 captures some aspects of their approach. Theoretically, concepts such as positive and negative feedback cycles, delay structures, and nonlinear relations are part of their vocabulary. Methodologically, they first ground themselves in real practical situations (e.g., examine TQM change and outcomes over time) and then mathematically formalize the relations, create a simulation of the critical paths, and compare the simulation to actual data. Their discipline in diagramming relations among variables is critical. I tried to illustrate that practice in the figures in this book.

These two methodological approaches bear on understanding organizational linkages. They start in a similar way by identifying a practical problem and qualitatively generating descriptive information. Vaughan (1996) drilled down into the basic information and elements of the situation. Sterman et al. (1997) abstracted from the setting and focused on formal understanding of the interplay of some critical interrelations among variables. In the Vaughan data set, a reader could use the data to reconstruct new leads and explore new paths. In the system dynamics simulation, one could pose alternative scenarios (e.g., what if Analog Devices raised or lowered their prices by X%) and look at possible outcomes.

Is there another option? Some researchers may shy away from "Challenger-like" research because of its time commitment and nonquantitative features. Others may shy away from the "system dynamics" approach, either because of the different skill set or different tastes associated with organizational research. Although I think these two options are very appropriate, there are other choices, namely, conducting a linkage analysis. I think of these as "focused investigations of linkages." "Focused" means they are much narrower in scope, limited in time, and geared to more specific hypotheses. Here are some examples:

Mining

Very early in this book, I acknowledged a mistake. My colleagues and I had done a very careful and formal job estimating the effects of organizational change (Epple et al., 1983) on group or section productivity but failed to ask whether it would have affected mine productivity. Actually, that extension would have been straightforward. We had estimated the productivity changes, knew the productivity data from all the other sections, and could have obtained mine-level productivity data. Estimating the impact of group- and mine-level changes was feasible. Therefore, in this focused problem, we could have explored productivity changes at one unit on the organizational unit.

Pizza Stores

In Chapter 8, I described a situation in which learning had occurred. I also knew when a majority of the stores had adopted the new cost-saving practice. Other practices were being shared and adopted to different degrees. Using the analytic techniques present in that study, it would be possible to estimate the impact of adopting cost-saving practices on the store cost function and then the relative contribution of store costs to corporate-level cost performance, that is, a limited linkage analysis could have been implemented.

Home Bakery Product

In Chapter 8, I examined the development of the new Home Bakery product. In the account by Nonaka and Takeuchi (1995), they argued that not only was the product successful, but it also generated other successful products. In linkage terms, activities and outcomes in the original product development team led to changes in division-level outcomes (new product revenue and profits), which led to the launching of new product development teams, which, in turn, positively affected division-level outcomes. Nonaka and Takeuchi called this "cross-leveling" of knowledge within and between divisions. A focused investigation of this topic might examine changes in basic values and beliefs within and across divisions. The assumption is that the success of the Home Bakery product changes tacit and explicit values and beliefs about the Easy and Rich concept or in the value of engineers working with customers. It is possible to test such an assumption. One could measure these values and beliefs of managers before and after the Home Bakery introduction and after other new product introductions. If direct measurement was not feasible, examining memos, proposals for new products, and speeches would be another way to observe whether values and beliefs were changing. This would be one limited way to determine whether impacts from one set of product activities were affecting the initiation of new products and their subsequent outcome.

Concluding Thoughts

- The question of how changes in activities and outcomes at one level affect activities and outcomes at other units or levels remains the basic theme.
- The linkage analysis tool box consists of
  — outcome coupling,
  — limiting conditions,
  — processes, and
  — feedback mechanisms.

  These tools can be used in the broad class of problems presented in Chapters 2 to 8. Only the emphasis may differ.

- A major value-added contribution of linkage analysis is to make explicit untested assumptions. If I think that improving group effectiveness should improve organizational effectiveness, let's make the linkages and related processes explicit. If we think that system-wide interventions improve individual-, group-, unit-, and organizational-level performance, let's make the linkages explicit.
- Another value-added contribution of linkage analysis is to frame new research problems. Discussions about the organizational change improvement paradox, the diminishing returns dilemma, the work concept dilemma, and the community of plants idea are illustrations of new research avenues.
- The concept of organizational mysteries was introduced to emphasize that tracing linkages across levels and units is a difficult and complicated task. Random trigger events, poor theories about time, and changing forms of organizing make linkage analysis a hard problem.

- Methodologically, there are some viable approaches that exist today and need not be invented. The existing methodological approaches for tracking linkages are
  — organizational detective work by Vaughan (1996),
  — system dynamics work by Sterman et al. (1997), and
  — focused linkage inquiry.

In conclusion, the challenge for me and for you, the reader, is to extend the linkage concept theoretically and empirically. There are hosts of untested organizational assumptions that we need to make more explicit. There are many new exciting organizational research problems stimulated by the linkage perspective. Hopefully, the tools presented in this book will provide a way to frame and to structure our understandings of these complicated cross-level phenomena. As we develop greater mastery about linkage issues, we will be better able to make sense of new forms of organizing in the future.

References

Adler, P. S., & Cole, R. E. (1993, Spring). Designed for learning: A tale of two auto plants. *Sloan Management Review*, pp. 85-94.

Argote, L. (1999). *Organizational learning and productivity: Creating, retaining and transferring knowledge.* Norwell, MA: Kluwer.

Argote, L., & Epple, D. (1990). Learning curves in manufacturing. *Science, 247,* 920-924.

Argyris, C. (1985). *Strategy, change and defensive routines.* Boston: Pitman.

Argyris, C. (1990). *Overcoming organizational defenses.* Boston: Allyn & Bacon.

Argyris, C., & Schon, D. A. (1978). *Organizational learning: A theory of action perspective.* Reading, MA: Addison-Wesley.

Attewell, P. A. (1994). Information technology and the productivity paradox. In D. H. Harris (Ed.), *Organizational linkages: Understanding the productivity paradox* (pp. 13-53). Washington, DC: National Academy Press.

Ault, R., Walton, R., & Childers, M. (1998). *What works: A decade of change at Champion International.* San Francisco: Jossey-Bass.

Bank of England. (1995, July 18). *Report of the Board of Banking Supervision Inquiry into the Circumstances of the Collapse of Barings.* London: Author.

Beer, M., Eisenstat, R. A., & Spector, B. (1990). Why change programs don't produce change. *Harvard Business Review, 68,* 158-166.

Berggren, C. (1994, Winter). Numi vs. Uddevalla. *Sloan Management Review,* pp. 37-45.

Boning, B., Ichniowski, C., & Shaw, K. (1998). *Incentive pay for production workers: An empirical analysis.* Manuscript in preparation, Columbia University.

Brown, J. S., & Duguid, P. (1991). Organizational learning and communities-of-practice: Toward a unified view of working, learning and innovation. *Organization Science, 2,* 40-57.

Cameron, K. S., & Whetten, D. A. (1983). *Organizational effectiveness: A comparison of multiple models.* San Diego, CA: Academic Press.

Cascio, W. F., Young, C. E., & Morris, J. R. (1997). Financial consequences of employment-change decisions in major U.S. corporations. *Academy of Management Journal, 40,* 1175-1189.

Chan, D. (1998). Functional relations among constructs in the same content domain at different levels: A typology of composition models. *Journal of Applied Psychology, 83,* 234-246.

Crown, D. F., & Rosse, J. G. (1995). Yours, mine, and ours: Facilitating group productivity through the integration of individual and group goals. *Organizational Behavior and Human Decision Processes, 64,* 138-150.

Cyert, R. M., & March, J. (1963). *A behavioral theory of the firm.* Englewood Cliffs, NJ: Prentice Hall.

Darr, E. D., Argote, L., & Epple, D. (1995). The acquisition, transfer, and depreciation of knowledge in service organizations: Productivity in franchises. *Management Science, 41,* 1750-1762.

Dean, J. W., & Goodman, P. S. (1993). *Toward a theory of total quality integration.* Unpublished manuscript, Kenan-Flagler Business School, University of North Carolina, Chapel Hill.

Deming, W. E. (1986). *Out of the crisis.* Cambridge: MIT Press.

Diehl, E., & Sterman, J. (1995). Effects of feedback complexity on dynamic decision making. *Organizational Behavior and Human Decision Processes, 62,* 198-215.

Epple, D., Argote, L., & Devadas, R. (1991). Organizational learning curves: A method for investigating intra-plant transfer of knowledge acquired through learning by doing. *Organization Science, 2,* 58-70.

Epple, D., Argote, L., & Murphy, K. (1996). An empirical investigation of the microstructure of knowledge acquisition and transfer through learning by doing. *Operations Research, 44,* 77-86.

Epple, D., Goodman, P. S., & Fidler, E. (1983). Assessing the economic consequences of organizational change. In S. Seashore (Ed.), *Assessing organizational change* (pp. 477-499). New York: John Wiley.

Fine, C. H. (1998). *Clockspeed : Winning industry control in the age of temporary advantage.* Reading, MA: Perseus.

Freeman, S. J., & Cameron, K. S. (1993). Organizational downsizing: A convergence and reorientation framework. *Organization Science, 4,* 10-29.

Gleick, J. (1987). *Chaos: Making a new science.* New York: Viking.

Goodman, P. S. (1979). *Assessing organizational change: The Rushton Quality of Work experiment.* New York: Wiley-Interscience.

Goodman, P. S. (Ed.). (1982). *Change in organizations.* San Francisco: Jossey-Bass.

Goodman, P. S., & Darr, E. D. (1996). Exchanging best practices through computer-aided systems. *Academy of Management Executive, 10,* 7-19.

Goodman, P. S., & Darr, E. D. (1998). Computer-aided systems and communities: Mechanisms for organizational learning in distributed environments. *MIS Quarterly, 22,* 417-440.

Goodman, P. S., Devadas, R., & Griffith Hughson, T. L. (1988). Groups and productivity: Analyzing the effectiveness of self-managing teams. In J. P. Campbell & R. J. Campbell (Eds.), *Productivity in organizations* (pp. 295-327). San Francisco: Jossey-Bass.

Goodman, P. S., Lerch, F. J., & Mukhopadhyay, T. (1994). Individual and organizational productivity: Linkages and processes. In D. H. Harris (Ed.), *Organizational link-*

ages: Understanding the productivity paradox (pp. 54-80). Washington, DC: National Academy Press.

Goodman, P. S., & Olivera, F. (1998, June). *Knowledge sharing in distributed environments*. Paper presented at Transfer of Knowledge and Levels of Learning conference, Carnegie Mellon University, Pittsburgh, PA.

Goodman, P. S., & Whetten, D. A. (1998). Fifty years of organizational behavior from multiple perspectives. In M. Neufeld & J. McKelvey (Eds.), *Industrial relations at the dawn of the new millennium* (pp. 33-53). Ithaca, NY: Cornell School of Industrial and Labor Relations.

Goodman, P. S., & Wilson, J. M. (1998, October). *New forms of work groups: Exocentric teams*. Paper presented at Robert B. McKersie Festschrift titled Negotiations and Change: From the Workplace to Society, Boston.

Hackman, J. R., & Oldham, G. R. (1980). *Work redesign*. Reading, MA: Addison-Wesley.

Hall, R. I. (1976). A system pathology of an organization: The rise and fall of the old *Saturday Evening Post. Administrative Science Quarterly, 21,* 185-211.

Harris, D. H. (1994). Productivity linkages in computer-aided design. In D. H. Harris (Ed.), *Organizational linkages: Understanding the productivity paradox* (pp. 240-261). Washington, DC: National Academy Press.

Haunschild, P. R., & Beckman, C. M. (1999). *Learning through networks: Effects of partner experience on acquisition premia*. Manuscript in preparation, Graduate School of Business, Stanford University, Palo Alto, CA.

Hollenbeck, J. R., Ilgen, D. R., LePine, J. A., Colquitt, J. A., & Hedlund, J. (1998). Extending the multilevel theory of team decision making: Effects of feedback and experience in hierarchical teams. *Academy of Management Journal, 41,* 269-282.

Huber, G. P. (1991). Organizational learning: The contributing processes and the literatures. *Organization Science, 2,* 88-115.

Ichniowski, C., & Shaw, K. (1999). The effects of human resource management systems on economic performance: An international comparison of U.S. and Japanese plants. *Management Science, 25,* 704-721.

Ingram, P., & Baum, J.A.C. (1997). Chain affiliation and the failure of Manhattan hotels. *Administrative Science Quarterly, 42,* 68-102.

Kaplan, R. S., & Norton, D. P. (1996). *The balanced scorecard: Translating strategy into action*. Boston: Harvard Business School Press.

Katz, D., & Kahn, R. L. (1966). *The social psychology of organizations*. New York: John Wiley.

Klein, K. J., Dansereau, F., & Hall, R. J. (1994). Levels issues in theory development, data collection, and analysis. *Academy of Management Review, 19,* 195-229.

Kozlowski, S.W.J., & Salas, E. (1997). A multilevel organizational systems approach for the implementation and transfer of training. In J. K. Ford (Ed.), *Improving training effectiveness in work organizations* (pp. 247-287). Hillsdale, NJ: Lawrence Erlbaum.

Kraut, R., Dumais, S., & Koch, S. (1989). Computerization, productivity, and quality of work-life. *Communications of the ACM, 32,* 220-238.

Lant, T. K., & Mezias, S. J. (1992). An organizational learning model of convergence and reorientation. *Organization Science, 3,* 47-71.

LaPorte, T. R., & Consolini, P. M. (1991, Winter). Working in practice but not in theory: Theoretical challenge of high reliability organizations. *Journal of Public Administration Research and Theory,* pp. 19-47.

Latane, B., & Darley, J. M. (1970). *The unresponsive bystander: Why doesn't he help?* Norwalk, CT: Appleton-Century-Crofts.

Laumann, E. O., Marsden, P. V., & Prensky, D. (1983). The boundary specification problem in network analysis. In R. S. Burt & M. J. Minor (Eds.), *Applied network analysis* (pp. 18-34). Beverly Hills, CA: Sage.

Lawler, E. E. (1986). *High involvement management.* San Francisco: Jossey-Bass.

Lawler, E. E. (1992). *The ultimate advantage.* San Francisco: Jossey-Bass.

Lawler, E. E. (1996). *From the ground up: Six principles for creating new logic organizations.* San Francisco: Jossey-Bass.

Lawler, E. E., Mohrman, S. A., & Ledford, G. E. (1998). *Strategies for high performance organizations.* San Francisco: Jossey-Bass.

MacDuffie, J. P. (1995). Human resource bundles and manufacturing performance: Organizational logic and flexible production systems in the world auto industry. *Industrial and Labor Relations Review, 48,* 197-221.

MacDuffie, J. P., & Pil, F. K. (1997). Changes in auto industry employment practices: An international overview. In T. A. Kochan, R. Lansbury, & J. P. MacDuffie (Eds.), *After lean production: Evolving employment practices in the world auto industry* (pp. 9-44). Ithaca, NY: Cornell University Press.

March, J. G. (1991). Exploration and exploitation in organizational learning. *Organization Science, 2,* 71-87.

McGrath, J. E. (1984). *Groups: Interaction and performance.* Englewood Cliffs, NJ: Prentice Hall.

Meyer, M. W., & Gupta, V. (1994). The performance paradox. In B. M. Staw & T. Cummings (Eds.), *Research in organizational behavior* (Vol. 16, pp. 309-369). Greenwich, CT: JAI.

Miner, A. S., & Mezias, S. J. (1996). Ugly duckling no more: Pasts and futures of organizational learning research. *Organization Science, 7,* 88-99.

Ministry of Finance. (1995). *Report of the inspectors of Barings Futures (Singapore) Pte Ltd. Singapore: Ministry of Finance, Government of Singapore.*

Mohrman, A. M., Mohrman, S. A, Ledford, G. E., Lawler, E. E., & Cummings, T. G. (1989). *Large scale organizational change.* San Francisco: Jossey-Bass.

Moreland, R. L. (1999). Transactive memory: Learning who knows what in work groups and organizations. In L. Thompson, D. Messick, & J. Levine (Eds.), *Shared cognition in organizations* (pp. 11-65). Mahwah, NJ: Lawrence Erlbaum.

Nadler, D. A., Gerstein, M. S., & Shaw, R. B. (1992). *Organizational architecture: Designs for changing organizations.* San Francisco: Jossey-Bass.

Nadler, D. A., Shaw, R. B., & Walton, A. E. (1995). *Discontinuous change.* San Francisco: Jossey-Bass.

National Transportation Safety Board. (1997, August 19). *Final report on in-flight fire and impact with terrain of ValuJet Airlines flight 592, DC-9-32, N904J, Everglades, Miami, Florida.* Washington, DC: Author. [Available on the Internet: http://www.ntsb.gov/Publictn/1997/AAR9706.htm]

Nonaka, I., & Takeuchi, H. (1995). *The knowledge-creating company: How Japanese companies create the dynamics of innovation.* New York: Oxford University Press.

Olivera, F., & Goodman, P. S. (1998, October). *Memory systems in organizations: Individuals' use of information about their firm's experience.* Paper presented at the INFORMS Conference on Knowledge, Knowing, and Organizations. Seattle, WA.

Parsons, T. (1951). *The social system.* New York: Free Press.

Perrow, C. (1984). *Normal accidents: Living with high risk systems.* New York: Basic Books.

Pfeffer, J. (1994). *Competitive advantage through people.* Boston: Harvard Business School Press.

Pfeffer, J., & Salancik, G. R. (1978). *The external control of organizations: A resource dependence perspective.* New York: Harper & Row.

Pil, F. K., & MacDuffie, J. P. (1996). The adoption of high-involvement work practices. *Industrial Relations, 35,* 423-455.

Pritchard, R. (1992). Organizational productivity. In M. D. Dunnette & L. M. Hough (Eds.), *Handbook in industrial and organizational psychology* (2nd ed., Vol. 3, pp. 443-471). Palo Alto, CA: Consulting Psychologists Press.

Ramanujam, R., & Goodman, P. S. (1998, August). *Reconceptualizing organizational errors.* Paper presented at the Academy of Management Meeting, San Diego, CA.

Repenning, N. P. (1997). *Successful change sometimes ends with results: Resolving the improvement paradox through computer simulation.* Manuscript in preparation, Sloan School of Management, Massachusetts Institute of Technology.

Roberts, K. H. (1990). Some characteristics of high reliability organizations. *Organization Science, 2,* 1-17.

Roberts, K. H., Hulin, C. L., & Rousseau, D. M. (1978). *Developing an interdisciplinary science of organizations.* San Francisco: Jossey-Bass.

Rousseau, D. M., & House, R. J. (1994). Meso organizational behavior: Avoiding three fundamental biases. In C. L. Cooper & D. M. Rousseau (Eds.), *Trends in organizational behavior* (pp. 13-30). New York: John Wiley.

Sagan, S. D. (1993). *The limits of safety: Organizations, accidents, and nuclear weapons.* Princeton, NJ: Princeton University Press.

Schneider, B., & Bowen, D. E. (1995). *Winning the service game.* Boston: Harvard Business School Press.

Schneider, B., & Klein, K. J. (1994). What is enough? A systems perspective on individual-organizational performance linkages. In D. H. Harris (Ed.), *Organizational linkages: Understanding the productivity paradox* (pp. 54-80). Washington, DC: National Academy Press.

Scott, W. R. (1995). *Institutions and organizations.* Thousand Oaks, CA: Sage.

Shrivastava, P. (1987). *Bhopal: Anatomy of a crisis.* Cambridge, MA: Ballinger.

Sitkin, S. B., Sutcliffe, K. M., & Schroeder, R. G. (1994). Distinguishing control from learning in total quality management: A contingency perspective. *Academy of Management Review, 19,* 537-564.

Sitkin, S. B., Sutcliffe, K. M., & Weick, K. E. (1998). Organizational learning. In R. C. Dorf (Ed.), *The technology management handbook* (pp. 70-76). Boca Raton, FL: CRC Press/Institute of Electrical and Electronics Engineers Press.

Sproull, L. S., & Hofmeister, K. R. (1986). Thinking about implementation. *Journal of Management, 12,* 43-60.

Staw, B. M. (1981). The escalation of commitment to a course of action. *Academy of Management Review, 6,* 577-587.

Sterman, J. D. (1994). Learning in and about complex systems. *Journal of the System Dynamics Society, 10,* 291-330.

Sterman, J. D., Repenning, N., & Kofman, F. (1997). Unanticipated side effects of successful quality programs: Exploring a paradox of organizational improvement. *Management Science, 43,* 503-521.

Susman, G. I. (1990). Work groups: Autonomy, technology, and choice. In P. S. Goodman & L. S. Sproull (Eds.), *Technology and organizations* (pp. 87-108). San Francisco: Jossey-Bass.

Thompson, J. D. (1967). *Organizations in action.* New York: McGraw-Hill.

Trist, E., Higgins, G., Murray, H., & Pollock, A. (1963). *Organizational choice.* London: Tavistock.

Van de Ven, A. H., & Drazin, R. (1985). Alternative forms of fit in congruency theory. *Administrative Science Quarterly, 30,* 514-539.

Vaughan, D. (1996). *The Challenger launch decision: Risky technology, culture, and deviance at NASA.* Chicago: University of Chicago Press.

Walton, R. E. (1987). *Innovating to compete.* San Francisco: Jossey-Bass.

Weick, K. E. (1979). *The social psychology of organizing.* Reading, MA: Addison-Wesley.

Weick, K. E. (1995). *Sensemaking in organizations.* Thousand Oaks, CA: Sage.

Weick, K. E., Sutcliffe, K., & Obstfeld, D. (1999). Organizing for high reliability: Processes of collective mindfulness. In B. Staw & R. Sutton (Eds.), *Research in organizational behavior* (Vol. 21, pp. 81-123). Greenwich, CT: JAI.

Weick, K. E., & Westley, F. (1996). Organizational learning: Affirming an oxymoron. In S. R. Clegg, C. Hardy, & W. R. Nord (Eds.), *Handbook of organization studies* (pp. 440-458). Thousand Oaks, CA: Sage.

Wellins, R. S., Byham, W. C., & Wilson, J. M. (1991). *Empowered teams: Creating self-directed work groups that improve quality, productivity, and participation.* San Francisco: Jossey-Bass.

Zager, R., & Rosow, M. P. (1982). *The innovative organization.* Elmsford, NY: Pergamon.

Index

About the Author

Paul S. Goodman is Professor of Industrial Administration and Psychology at the Graduate School of Industrial Administration at Carnegie Mellon University, in Pittsburgh, Pennsylvania. He received his B.A. degree in economics from Trinity College, his M.B.A. degree from Dartmouth College, and his Ph.D. degree in organizational psychology from Cornell University. His research interests are in work groups, knowledge sharing, technology, and organizational change. His current research focuses on new forms of groups, organizational linkages, knowledge sharing, and organizational errors. His writings appear in many professional journals and books. He is a fellow in the American Psychological Society and the Society for Industrial and Organizational Psychology. He is the Co-Director of the Center for the Management of Technology, which conducts applied research projects with industry, and the Director of the Institute for Strategic Development, which develops strategic partnerships in Mexico, Latin America, India, and South Africa. In addition, he produces a video series about the "Changing Nature of Work."